Teaching
the Emotionally
Disturbed
A CASEBOOK

Herbert Grossman
Hawthorne Cedar Knolls School

HOLT, RINEHART and WINSTON, Inc.
New York · *Chicago* · *San Francisco* · *Toronto* · *London*

When the author first began to teach the emotionally disturbed, he found little help in the books available on the subject. Containing little more than broad generalizations about emotionally disturbed persons and techniques appropriate to teaching them as a group, these books failed to reflect the variety of educational and emotional problems that disturbed students exhibit. For help in understanding his students as individuals, the author turned to the science of psychology.

Although writings on the emotionally disturbed have become more plentiful in recent years, they do not yet deal adequately with the uniqueness of the disturbed person and with the educational implications of that uniqueness. This book attempts, through integrating relevant methods and techniques of both education and psychology, to help those who teach and work with the emotionally disturbed to focus on the differences rather than the similarities among their students.

Concentrating on the individual, it employs a case study approach to provide a frame of reference for applying the insights of psychology to individual problems in order to determine which of many educational techniques are most appropriate for a given student. With this in mind, the author uses the case studies to demonstrate some of the ways in which social histories, psychological reports, school reports, and similar materials can provide the information necessary in making such decisions. Because factors other than the personality of the student must be considered in deciding how to deal with his problems, the author also suggests ways in which such elements as the structure and policy of the school, the availability of an interdisciplinary team approach, and the nature of the group within which the student lives can be taken into account during the decision-making process. The teacher-pupil relationship is stressed throughout the book for several reasons: first, because many of the problems of emotionally disturbed students are reflected in their relationships with their teachers and others; second, because many of the educational difficulties of disturbed students can best be dealt with through appropriate teacher-pupil relationships; and finally, because problems in teacher-pupil relationships are often the most difficult for educators to overcome.

Because the book has a rather unusual format, a few words about its organization may be helpful. The first chapter introduces the case studies and describes the setting in which they were obtained. Chapter Two outlines broadly a frame of reference for using the principles of psychology to achieve an understanding of disturbed behavior in terms of the emotional problems that underlie it. In Chapters Three through Five, this frame of reference is applied to the case studies of three students who exemplify three broad categories of emotional disturbance. The case studies are analyzed in a manner that emphasizes the individual characteristics of each student's personality; the analyses are analogous to the process by which an educator might attempt to understand his own students in his own specific environment. Included in sections of comment, these analyses are intended to illustrate a process rather than to provide definitive answers.

In Chapter Six, general principles about the education of emotionally disturbed students are induced from the individual case studies. These principles concern dimensions of personality along which disturbed students differ and the educational implications of these dimensions, the contribution of the interdisciplinary team to the achievement of educational goals, the contribution of the teacher to the achievement of the goals of total rehabilitation, the relative amenability of various educational problems to educational rather than psychotherapeutic solution, and the pitfalls that confront educators in their attempts to deal with students' educational difficulties.

Guidelines for determining what curriculum, class size, grouping, and other elements are most appropriate to typical educational difficulties of disturbed students are also induced from the case studies. Because of the author's belief in the importance of the *process* of understanding the student, he has included in the final chapter a case study that is not followed by comment. The reader is encouraged to analyze this study as though he were the student's teacher, seeking to understand the student's difficulties. The final chapter contains also questions for further thought and discussion that highlight some of the major ideas dealt with in the text.

The reader will note, of course, that the students described in the case studies do not typify all emotionally disturbed students and that their residential setting does not represent all educational environments. Nevertheless, the conceptual frame of reference, the process suggested for understanding the behavior and the problems of these students, and the guidelines for selecting techniques with which to deal with them are applicable to other students in other settings.

It is impossible to acknowledge here the assistance of all those who have contributed to the preparation of this book. I wish to express my grateful appreciation to the Jewish Board of Guardians and to the staff of the Hawthorne Cedar Knolls School, without whose cooperation this book could not have been written. Mr. Herschel Alt, Mr. Jerome Goldsmith, and Mr. Harry Krohn of these agencies were the individuals directly responsible for affording me this cooperation. The reports of Dr. Albert Karafin and Mr. Jerome Rosenberg comprise much of the case material. Dr. Howard Polsky and Mr. Frank Willie helped me to clarify the theoretical approach. I am indebted also to Dr. Frances Connor and to the many students of the Special Education Department of Teachers College, Columbia University, for invaluable comment on earlier forms of the manuscript. Miss Annette Koshut and Mrs. Helene Aarons did Herculean jobs in editing and typing the initial manuscript. My wife's patience and encouragement made the improbable possible.

New York City   H. G.
March 1963

contents

chapter 1

Introduction

PURPOSE

In recent years there has been an ever-increasing demand for educators trained to work with emotionally disturbed students. This increased demand has originated from two sources. Foremost of these has been the expansion of the various educational services required by emotionally disturbed students, such as residential treatment centers, special day schools, special classes within the community school, and additional services for the disturbed student in the regular classroom. The second and most recent source has been the growing realization that many students who are physically handicapped, mentally retarded, brain-damaged, culturally deprived, or delinquent also have serious emotional problems which impede their educational progress. In part, because of the relative recency of their programs, the universities which have risen to the challenge of training educators to work with disturbed students have not as yet come to any shared agreement about what should comprise adequate preparation for the field.

Their training programs usually include the development of both a firm foundation in good educational practices which are applicable to all students and a psychological understanding of the special problems of emotionally disturbed students.

This book is written to provide the educator with a way of integrating these two disciplines under the assumption that the educational technique of choice for many learning and behavioral difficulties depends to an extent on the emotional problem underlying them. It sets out to accomplish its goal of integration by providing the educator with one way of applying, to disturbed educational behavior, the insights of psychology. This is not meant to transform the educator into a clinician. Rather, it is meant to provide him with the conceptual tools for culling from the mass of data which surround him that which is pertinent for sound educational decisions.

OVERVIEW

The following chapter presents a frame of reference for viewing disturbed educational behavior dynamically in terms of the emotional problems which help create it. This frame of reference is used in subsequent chapters to analyze educational case studies of three students who exemplify three broad categories of emotional disturbance. Each student's case study is analyzed in a way which underscores those of his **unique** personality characteristics which have implications for the selection of educational techniques to deal with his educational difficulties. **General** principles about the education of emotionally disturbed students are induced from the **individual** case studies in a chapter which follows them. These include generalizations about dimensions of personality along which emotionally disturbed students differ and which have important educational implications, pitfalls which confront educators in their attempts to deal effectively with their students' educational difficulties, the educator's contribution to the interdisciplinary team's efforts to rehabilitate emotionally disturbed students, the team's contributions to the educator's educational efforts, and the relative amenability of various educational difficulties to educational rather than psychotherapeutic solutions. Guidelines for employing curriculum, class-size, groupings, and other educational techniques to deal with typical educational difficulties of emotionally disturbed students are also induced from the case studies.

The final chapter consists of an unanalyzed educational case study which the reader is encouraged to analyze. Additional questions are raised in order to highlight some of the major ideas dealt with in the text.

THE CASE STUDIES

The Choice of Students

The students, two teen-age girls and one teen-age boy, who are the subjects of the case studies presented in Chapters 3–5, all lived in a residential treatment center during the time the material in the case studies was prepared. These three were chosen primarily because they represent the three major dynamically different categories of emotional disturbances which have meaning for the educator. They were also chosen because they were in virtually the same classes and shared almost the same teachers. Thus the reader should be able to discern which aspects of their behavior depended more on their unique personality characteristics and which depended more on environmental circumstances. The reader should also be able to discern which of their teachers' reactions depended primarily on their own personality characteristics and which depended more on the uniqueness of each student. Finally, because of a fortuitous circumstance, namely, that the students were in noncoeducational classes which were later combined, the reader is able to explore the effects of heterosexual groupings on their behavior.

The Teachers

The three educators whose anecdotal reports are included in the case studies were all licensed teachers. None of them had received clinical training. Two of them had had very little experience with emotionally disturbed children. Perhaps, if they had been more experienced, they would have reacted differently to their students' disturbed behavior and there would have been fewer educational difficulties in the anecdotal reports to analyze. Since they were not experienced, their reports give the reader some idea of the kinds of pitfalls which are likely to confront a relatively inexperienced educator.

The School

The school which the students attended was an "on-grounds," independent school district which functioned as part of a residential treatment center. The description of the school which follows was characteristic of it at the time when the students in the case studies were in attendance.

There were approximately two hundred students ranging in age from eight to eighteen. Although it was small compared to many school districts, it nevertheless offered an extremely varied program to the students. The high school program consisted of academic, vocational training, and terminal education tracks. The academic track in which the three students were enrolled offered world geography, world history, and American history; English, nine through eleven; algebra and geometry; general science, biology, and earth science; French; commercial subjects; beauty culture; homemaking; art; music; and gym. Students could also choose from an extensive list of industrial art courses. Remedial education, tutorial classes, and study halls were also available. Class size varied from six to sixteen. Although all students were required to attend classes, the variety of tracks and subjects enabled them to enroll in courses which reflected their professed interests.

The educational philosophy of the school was the same as that of most schools: "Starting with the student at his level, with a sound knowledge of maturational and developmental growth factors, the school aimed to develop skill, impart knowledge, stimulate interests, cultivate special abilities, and enhance self-esteem." The overall policy of the school was to provide the best possible education and the most normal school atmosphere that the students' difficulties would allow. When deviations from the normal were required by a student's emotional problems, they were thought of as temporary necessities to be abolished as soon as possible.

The Institution

The residential treatment center of which the school was a part was situated on the outskirts of a large city from which it accepted most of its youngsters. However, students from suburbs, other parts of the state, and other states were also in residence. Referrals were accepted from children's courts, departments of welfare, and private agencies, with referrals by courts comprising slightly more than 50 percent of the total. The major criteria for admission were an ability to tolerate an open door or unlocked setting, and an inability to be treated in a nonresidential setting.

The treatment services offered to the students included those of psychiatrists, psychologists, and psychiatric social workers. Each student was assigned to a junior, intermediate, or senior unit, depending on his age and social-emotional maturity. He lived in a cottage with a group of students his own age which was staffed by a married couple, called cottage parents. He was assigned to a psychiatric social worker who was his psychotherapist and he was also seen periodically by the unit psychiatrist. Almost all students were seen for initial psychological testing. Many were retested during their stay at the institution.

The treatment program was based on psychoanalytic principles. It emphasized both psychoanalytically oriented individual psychotherapy and milieu therapy, or planned living experiences. An interdisciplinary team-treatment approach was fostered by both periodic interdisciplinary progress meetings about each child and informal day-to-day communication between disciplines.

Content of the Case Studies

Each case study is divided into two parts. The first part begins with the background information which was available prior to the student's admission. This consists of an intake summary which contains information about the student's developmental and social history, summaries of separate interviews with the student and his parents, a report of his recent functioning in school, and the results of any recent psychological testing. The first part also contains information about the initial period of the student's stay at the institution. This includes reports of initial psychiatric interviews, psychological testing, interdisciplinary progress meetings, school functioning, and psychotherapy sessions.

The second part consists of information obtained during the following academic year. Teachers' periodic anecdotal reports make up the major portion of this section: reports of progress meetings, psychotherapy sessions, and additional psychological testing are also included when available and pertinent.

In many cases, extracts of pertinent material rather than complete reports are presented. Except for minor editorial changes and additions to clarify the intent of the reports for the reader, the material is presented as it was written.

Analysis of the Case Studies

The analysis of each case simulates the procedure the reader might follow if he were confronted with the student at the point in time described in the materials. Four questions are raised about the material in the first part of each case study.

1. What are the student's major underlying problems?

2. What techniques does he use to cope with these problems, and how successful are they?

3. What kinds of educational difficulties are his problems likely to create?

4. What important factors should the educator consider when deciding how to handle these educational difficulties, if they occur?

In answering these questions, the reports of psychiatric interviews and psychological tests are used primarily to discover the student's underlying emotional problems. School reports and intake summaries are mainly used to provide information about the techniques he uses to cope with his problems and his success at doing so. Although psychotherapy summaries are used to provide information about all these questions, they are included primarily to illustrate the psychotherapist's contribution to the student's educational progress.

Two basic questions are applied to the teacher's anecdotal reports in the second part.

1. What educational difficulties resulted from the problems which were noted in the first part?

2. How might the educator attempt to lessen these difficulties?

Additional questions are raised about the appropriateness of the methods which the teachers employed to ameliorate the student's difficulties and about the kinds of educational experiences for which the student might be best suited during the following year.

Although the author's own answers to these questions are included, the reader is encouraged to react to the questions before reading them. In the long run, the experience of responding to the questions may prove more valuable to the reader than the author's analyses of the case studies. The reader may believe that the case studies provide him with enough information to formulate hypotheses about the development of the student's emotional problems. The material is not used in this way in the case studies because the focus of the text is on understanding the student's disturbed behavior at a moment in time, not as a result of a developmental history. However, the reader is encouraged to use the material in whatever manner he wishes.

chapter 2

Conceptualizing Emotionally Disturbed Behavior

VIGNETTES

The following vignettes of emotionally disturbed students were written by their teachers. They serve to identify the kinds of students and the behavior with which this books deals. They also provide the material from which examples will be drawn to illustrate the concepts discussed in this chapter.

Helen

Helen is an extremely isolated student who almost never speaks to any of her peers. She never volunteers and when I ask her a question she responds in a faint, almost inaudible whisper. During the coed recess period she remains alone in the classroom. She has never removed her coat even on the warmest days because she wants to hide her extreme obesity. Helen follows every classroom procedure to the letter. However, although she completes all her grammar, vocabulary, and spelling assignments, she refuses to write compositions, discuss

9

literature, or reveal her opinions about anything. She is extremely uncommunicative and unemotional. When I try to exert pressure on her to participate more in class, she refuses in an excessively polite manner.

Paul

Paul is an extremely hostile youngster. He constantly provokes the other students by his nasty comments. When any of them retaliate he loses control of himself and has to be restrained forcibly. There are two weak students whom he uses as his personal scapegoats whenever he comes into the class in an angry mood. I am quite annoyed by his tendency to undermine my authority by telling disorderly students to behave. If I ask him in front of the others not to do this, he flies into a rage. When I discuss it with him privately he claims that I am picking on him and accusing him unjustly. He seems to believe that he is really trying to help me keep the class under control.

Paul likes to joke with me in class. At first I encouraged it in the hope of developing a better relationship with him. However, without his realizing it, his jokes soon became quite abusive and I had to put a stop to them.

Jim

Jim is an extremely disorganized youngster. He loses everything I give him, forgets to bring his books to class, and even forgets to hand work in at the end of the period. He used to spend most of the period out of contact with classroom activities, daydreaming. I noticed him smiling and laughing about his daydreams. Now that he is more attuned to the class, we are engaged in a constant power struggle because he wants to do the opposite of what I ask. He wants to put his own heading on his work, hand in assignments on different days, hang up his coat in a different place, call me by a different name, and so on. Actually, this is a big improvement over his previous behavior because now he is more involved in what is going on in class.

John

It is extremely difficult to find suitable curriculum material for John because, although his academic skills are quite limited, his interests are commensurate with his age. His initial reluctance to acknowledge his academic difficulties compounded the problem, for even when I found such materials, he would not use them. Whenever I asked him to do something which required him to reveal his inadequacies he refused. To be sure, he answered "Yes" or "Of course," but he did so merely to placate me. Cajoling him, reasoning with him, or exerting pressure on him had no effect on his unwillingness to face his deficiencies. He even played the part of a mature, capable, intellectual adult to the point of keeping a pipe conspicuously in his shirt pocket in order to hide his feelings of inadequacy.

Eventually John revealed his true feelings to me. After the class had read "Of Mice and Men" he confided in me that he could really understand how Lennie felt because Lennie's stupidity reminded him of himself. On another occasion, after we had read a play in which the hero was a mentally retarded adult, he made a similar comment. He told me that when he read the hero's diary it was the first time he was able to read anything without becoming upset because the hero had made the same kinds of spelling and grammatical errors that he himself does. These feelings of inadequacy may account for his almost constant state of depression.

John has little to do with the other students in the class. They try to provoke him by ridiculing his deficiencies, but to no avail. He tells them that they are too childish and immature to bother him.

Margaret

Margaret is a girl of contrasts. She constantly looks annoyed and displeased, but when I speak to her she smiles pleasantly regardless of what I say. She is very bright and quick to learn, but her ideas about the world are full of distortions.

During the early part of the term she would not admit that she needed to wear a hearing aid. She did not hear much of what went on in class because she did not wear one. When other students recited or when I showed narrated films, she was especially handicapped because her modest ability to read lips was useless. The effects of her refusal to wear a hearing aid were apparent in her distorted conceptions of the material we had covered. Margaret's work improved tremendously when she began to use her hearing aid. However, this lasted only a few weeks. She refused to continue to wear it and her functioning deteriorated markedly.

Donald

Donald is extremely impulsive and impatient. When he knows an answer, he blurts it out because he cannot wait to be called on. If he is asked to do something he begins before he is told how to do it. As soon as he has difficulty with a problem, he quits. He says whatever comes into his mind no matter how foolish or mean it is.

Donald is extremely fearful in class. Whenever a new topic is broached he becomes convinced that he cannot master it and must be given immediate reassurance that he can. Last week he ran out of class during an examination, screaming that the work was too easy and too boring and that I did not know how to teach. He has been cutting classes recently. When he does come he is too restless to remain for the full period. Now he brings comic books to class with him in order to have something to read when he cannot concentrate. The classroom pressures are definitely too much for him.

Larry

Larry is an inveterate flatterer. He constantly tells me that I am a good teacher, an excellent baseball player, an understanding person, and so on. When he asks or answers a question he prefaces his remarks with such comments as "I am embarrassed to ask you but I am so stupid" or "Please don't feel bad if I do not understand. It is not your fault I am stupid." He is quite committed to perceiving himself in this way. Even when he performs well he belittles his achievement and refuses to acknowledge it.

It has been difficult for me to set appropriate goals for Larry because his mild brain damage affects his intellectual functioning unevenly. Since he performs adequately in some areas I tend to assume that he can do as well in others. In addition, it is not always possible to determine when his poor achievement is due to brain damage rather than to lack of effort.

NEED FOR A FRAME OF REFERENCE

The students described above had emotional problems which interfered with their educational functioning. Many of their educational difficulties occurred because they behaved in ways which limited their educational achievement in order to assuage the fear, anger, anxiety, and shame which disturbed them. The special task of the educator who works with such students is to help them cope with their disturbing emotions in ways which do not impede their educational progress.

This is not an easy task. The educator is often unaware of his students' feelings because much of their behavior is designed to conceal their disturbing emotions. Helen's masklike smile and John's play-acting the role of an intellectual adult were examples of this kind of behavior. Even when their behavior is not designed to conceal their emotions, the educator may still have difficulty fathoming their feelings because the same behavior may be the result of many different emotions. For instance, the student who indignantly complains that his teacher does not trust him because he was asked if he did his homework by himself may be acting indignantly because he feels guilty about copying his work, angry at being falsely accused, or fearful of the possible consequences of whatever he has actually done. In addition, the same emotion can result in superficially dissimilar behavior. A student who has actually copied his homework, and feels guilty about having done so when he is confronted by his teacher, may indignantly maintain his innocence, unemotionally promise not to copy again, or tearfully plead for forgiveness.

These examples underscore the educator's need for a frame of reference for going beyond the student's superficial behavior to the disturbing emotions which underlie it. Providing one such frame of reference is the major purpose of this book.

A frame of reference for understanding emotionally disturbed classroom behavior should help the educator recognize the emotion underlying the behavior and the factors arousing the emotion. This will help the educator avoid arousing disturbing emotions in his students and it will facilitate his attempts to encourage them to use more educationally desirable methods of coping with disturbing emotions when they do arise.

THE AROUSAL OF UPSETTING EMOTIONS

The classroom behavior of emotionally disturbed students is affected by disturbing emotions which arise both in and out of the classroom.

Out-of-Class Experiences

Emotionally disturbed students often enter the classroom already emotionally upset. They are susceptible to chronic feelings of depression, anxiety, anger, and so on, and are easily upset by experiences in their daily lives which normal students can take in stride. Once upset, they are more likely to continue to be so even when they have arrived in school. In the anecdotal material presented earlier, Margaret's constant annoyance, John's ever-present depression, and Paul's periods of anger are examples of disturbing emotional states probably not related to the immediate classroom situation.

The educator who does not recognize when his students' disturbing emotions are unrelated to classroom events is less likely to deal effectively with them. If he also assumes that he should be able to manage his students' emotions by manipulating their environment, he may create additional problems by reproaching himself for not accomplishing the impossible.

Classroom Experiences

Emotionally disturbed students are also likely to be affected by disturbing emotions which arise in the classroom itself. Being in the classroom can be a threatening experience for students with emotional problems. Many of them have not acquired the educational skills necessary to meet the educational demands imposed upon them. In addition, their emotional problems interfere with their ability to use even those skills they have developed. It is quite understandable that because of their poor **taskability,** that is, their limited ability to accomplish the educational tasks imposed upon them, they feel threatened when confronted with educational challenges. Even when they have the skills necessary to meet the challenges imposed upon them they often become upset because emotionally disturbed behavior is more likely to be the result of distortions and misperceptions of the classroom situation. Emotionally disturbed students, like their normal counterparts, tend to perceive their present and future in terms of their past. Unfortunately they also act on their generalizations regardless of their accuracy. When such students feel threatened by the challenge of novel educational tasks, it is more likely that they are responding to ill-founded anticipations of failure than to accurate appraisals of their taskability. Donald's need for immediate reassurance that he could master new tasks when he was confronted with them was the result of such ill-founded anticipations.

Emotionally disturbed students tend to distort and misperceive many aspects of the classroom situation. However, distorted perceptions of others are probably the most troublesome ones. Students may misperceive the requests of a nonpunitive, nonauthoritarian teacher as an attempt to inflict his will upon them; they may feel rejected by a sympathetic and interested teacher's comment that although he cannot help them at the moment, he would be pleased to spend some time with them after class; or they may believe that the concerned teacher who points out their deficiencies does so because he delights in rubbing salt in their wounds.

Such interpersonal distortions have been labeled **transferences** because the misperceiver transfers attributes he has perceived in others in his past to people in his present. **Transference** impedes the students' educational progress in many ways. It may interfere with the educator's attempt to convince mistrustful students either by words or by deeds that he is worthy of their trust. It may also lead some students to continue to demand inordinate amounts of sympathy from their teachers long after it is obvious to others that it will not be forthcoming.

One of the most important differences between emotionally disturbed and normal students is that the behavior of emotionally disturbed students is more affected by transferences and other factors which are irrelevant to, or are misperceptions of, the classroom situation. Unfortunately, these are just the factors least subject to the educator's control.

TECHNIQUES FOR
COPING WITH DISTURBING EMOTIONS

The educator of emotionally disturbed students faces a formidable task in his attempt to discern the emotions underlying his students' behavior. As noted above, his students may employ the same behavior to cope with a variety of emotions. Moreover, as we shall see below, their behavior is often actually designed to camouflage their emotional states. The educator needs to be aware of the sometimes intricate and often devious ways in which emotionally disturbed students cope with their emotions so that he will not be misled by their behavior.

INTERPERSONAL COPING TECHNIQUES

One of the ways in which students can assuage their disturbing emotions is by modifying their environment. In order to do this they usually have to induce a change in their teachers: changes in the status quo of the classroom often require action by or evoke reactions from the teacher in charge. In addition, the teacher is often the aspect of the environment which contributes most to the arousal of their disturbing emotions.

Three Modes of Interpersonal Relationships

The interpersonal techniques—maneuvers which emotionally disturbed students employ to bring about desired reactions from others—fall into three categories or modes: moving against others, moving toward others, and moving away from others. All students use techniques which fall into all categories. However, many students rely primarily on one mode of interpersonal relationship, regardless of whether that kind of relationship is appropriate for the specific situation.

Moving against others. Students who constantly attack, provoke, accuse, and blame others rely primarily and excessively on moving against others in order to cope with their emotions. Their actions tell us that they believe that others are poised to attack them and that their best defense is a good offense. Paul's teacher's description of his behavior affords an excellent example of the way such students behave. Students who move against others disrupt the class and annoy their teachers. Therefore, their behavior is likely to be viewed as disturbed behavior and to receive prompt attention.

Moving toward others. Students who move toward others in dealing with their problems are often rigidly conforming, polite, friendly, and cooperative. These students do not behave this way because they appreciate the need for cooperation with others or have a feeling of regard for them, but for other reasons. They may feel weak and powerless and want to curry favor from those whose aid they believe they must have. Or they may be terrified that others are ready to attack them and want to ward off the impending blows by their ingratiating behavior. Larry's predictable flattery and self-effacing comments epitomized this kind of behavior. Margaret's affectation of a masklike smile was a less extreme form of the same approach to people.

Since students who behave this way do so to please others, the educator is less likely to recognize that their behavior is disturbed. He may fail to see the disturbing emotions which drive the students to behave in their rigid and inflexible ways and he may not realize how it interferes with their educational progress.

Moving away from others.   Students whose interpersonal techniques consist primarily of moving away from others are usually characterized by daydreaming, an unwillingness to participate in discussions or to reveal their feelings, physical detachment from others, and a general reluctance to engage in interpersonal relationships. In the anecdotal material Jim the daydreamer and Helen the extreme isolate both relied on this mode of interpersonal relationship to an excessive degree.

This kind of behavior is disturbed behavior when it reflects a desire to avoid or escape not from a real threat but from an imagined one. It is educationally undesirable when students shrink away from the educational challenges necessary for educational achievement.

This behavior often goes uncorrected. Although it impedes the student's educational progress, it usually does not interfere with the group's functioning nor does it necessitate a confrontation between teacher and student. However, it may actually be the most undesirable mode of interpersonal relationship because it indicates that the student is more detached from and more estranged from people than he would be if he moved toward or even against others.

The educator who is aware that his students rely on one mode of interpersonal relationship to an excessive degree has already made a giant step toward discerning the disturbed emotions which underlie their behavior because he is aware that their behavior is disturbed.

DEFENSIVE COPING TECHNIQUES

Thus far in the discussion of the ways in which emotionally disturbed students cope with their disturbing emotions we have considered only interpersonal techniques. Another group of coping techniques, **defense mechanisms,** still remains to be considered. Defense mechanisms are maneuvers students employ to keep their disturbing emotions out of awareness. They differ from interpersonal techniques in two important respects. First, they are not designed to have an effect on or to evoke a reaction from others, although they may do so indirectly. Second, they are not employed to change the situation but to distort it or the threatening emotions it evokes. There are many defense mechanisms a student can employ to belie his disturbing emotions. Those most likely to create educational difficulties are considered in this section.

Repression

Repression, one of the most basic defense mechanisms, is the process of preventing a troubling thought and the discomforting emotion it would evoke from coming into awareness. In the classroom it is seen when students conveniently forget threatening matters, and when they forget to consider important aspects of complex personal issues and thereby find easy but inappropriate solutions to them.

Repression enables emotionally troubled students to avoid thinking about their problems; it also enables them to forget some of their responsibilities. The results of repression in the classroom, like the results of any defense mechanism, are not necessarily desirable or undesirable. They depend on whether the repressed ideas and emotions would have led to behavior which would have facilitated or impeded a student's educational progress.

Denial

Another way in which emotionally disturbed students defend themselves from threatening ideas and emotions is to deny or distort the reality which would evoke them. Almost any aspect of the classroom environment can be subject to denial. Some students who are committed to perceiving adults as hostile and threatening may deny the accepting and supporting actions of their teachers. Others may be committed to perceiving adults as supportive and deny their hostile actions. Some students may believe they are extraordinarily excellent students and deny their errors. Others may believe they cannot succeed and therefore deny their accomplishments.

When the student denies some aspect of the classroom situation he and his teacher are truly unable to agree on reality. Too often neither is able to believe that the other actually perceives the situation differently: both assume that the other is lying and react accordingly.

In the anecdotal material above, Margaret's inability to acknowledge her hearing loss and Larry's inability to accept his accomplishments were examples of denial. It was as if both said, "I cannot feel threatened because nothing is threatening me."

Reaction Formation

In reaction formation the students belie their feelings by acting contrary to them. Students who yearn for their teachers' approval may act as if their teachers' opinions have no significance at all; students who are ashamed of their physical handicaps may flaunt them; and students who feel inferior and inadequate may establish unrealistically high goals for themselves. It is as if they are saying: We do not want our teachers' approval. We are not ashamed of our handicap. We do not believe that we are inadequate. How can we when our actions refute such notions?

In the anecdotal material Helen's extreme politeness when she was pressed to participate and Margaret's masklike smile were probably reaction formations against anger.

Displacement

Displacement is the process of experiencing and acting out emotions, not in the situations which engender them but in an unrelated situation. The individual displaces his response from the situation in which the emotion is aroused because the response would be too threatening to one in which the response is more acceptable. For example, emotionally disturbed students may vent their anger not toward the bullies who evoke it, but against the weaker students in the group.

Paul's tendency to torture two of his peers whenever he was angry is an excellent illustration of displacement in action.

The educator who is bewildered by the displacement reactions of his students may be unable to account for their behavior. A given student's emotions will probably be quite apparent, but the cause of his emotions may remain concealed.

Rationalization

By rationalizing it emotionally disturbed students often defend themselves from the emotional threat their behavior would evoke: they interpret their behavior in ways more acceptable to them by attributing a major role to motives which had only a minor part in the genesis of their behavior. Paul's belief that he told his peers how to behave in order to aid and not hinder his teacher's efforts to control the class and Donald's belief that the reason he was having difficulty with the work was that it was too easy and too boring were rationalizations. It is as if each was saying, "Why should I be upset by my actions? There are good reasons for me to act as I do. Besides I am not doing anything wrong."

The educator has much more difficulty dealing with students who rationalize their behavior than with students who perceive their actions accurately. For the rationalizers are certain there is nothing to be modified or corrected.

RESULTS OF DEFENSE MECHANISMS

Defensive behavior can facilitate or impede educational progress. Students can deny their handicaps and succeed or deny their abilities and fail. Reaction formation can belie students' insecurities or their desires to succeed. Rationalization can be used to excuse delinquent behavior by students who wish to perceive themselves as compliant and cooperative. It can also make conforming behavior more palpable to the student who wishes to see himself as a delinquent.

Students employ defense mechanisms in order to avoid threatening emotions. They hide their feelings from themselves and in the process from their teachers as well. The educator observes the behavior that is an end product. He cannot observe the distorted perceptions or hidden feelings behind the behavior. Thus he is vulnerable to the kinds of mistaken notions about his students' behavior which can lead him to err in dealing with their educational difficulties.

He may assume that their defensive behavior accurately reflects their underlying emotions and proceed erroneously. If he is unaware of the real fear and anxiety which their reaction formations hide, he may encourage them to venture into ominous territory. If he fails to perceive the guilt which is hidden behind their defensive maneuvers, he may force them to acknowledge more guilt than they are able to accept.

He may assume mistakenly that the effects which their defenses have upon him accurately reflect the purposes for which they were intended. For example, when students deny and distort reality in order to cope with threatening emotions the obvious discrepancies between his perceptions of reality and theirs may lead him to believe that the students are trying to pull the wool over his eyes. When students displace their reactions on to him he may perceive them to be directed to him personally.

In order to avoid such errors the educator must base his educational decisions not on the defensive barriers which the students erect to keep their emotions hidden, but upon the emotions themselves. If he fails to do this, he risks the danger of allowing his students' emotional disturbances to disturb his relations with them.

SUMMARY

Students with emotional problems often have difficulties in school because they may behave in ways which limit their educational achievement in order to assuage their disturbing emotions. The special task of the educator of emotionally disturbed students is to discourage this emotionally disturbed behavior. He can do this by modifying the classroom situation so that it does not evoke as many disturbing emotions and by encouraging the students to use more educationally desirable methods of assuaging such emotions when they do arise. The educator must respond to his students' underlying emotions, not their superficial behavior. If he does not, he risks the danger of compounding the problems already created by his students' emotional problems.

This is an extremely difficult task for the educator to accomplish. Many of the factors which evoke his students' disturbing emotions are irrelevant to or distortions of the classroom situation.

In addition, the students' true emotional states are often difficult to discern. They tend to relate to their teachers in one interpersonal mode regardless of their feelings and employ defense mechanisms which conceal their emotions from themselves and others.

CONCLUDING COMMENTS

Can the educator of emotionally disturbed students actually determine why they behave as they do? Can he untangle the webs of transferences, defenses, and interpersonal techniques which mask their true feelings? Although this is a difficult and challenging task, it is not an impossible one.

The educator is a member of a team of professionals who can facilitate his efforts. The students' educational records provide him with information about their past functioning, their present taskability, and how they are likely to perceive educational challenges. Psychological tests and psychiatric reports, when available, provide him with clues about the kinds of emotions which may disturb his students and the ways in which they tend to deal with them. Comparing his observations of his students with the observations of others can help him to discover the transferences and distortions which affect their behavior.

Moreover, the educator can try out "alternative understandings" of his students' behavior. He can disregard sterile hypotheses and keep fruitful ones. There is seldom "a fatal error" which would destroy his relationship with his students. The significant factor is not the number of inappropriate responses the educator makes to his students, but the number of appropriate ones.

RECOMMENDED READINGS

Dollard and Miller's *"Personality and Psychotherapy"* (1950) contains an excellent description of the effects on behavior of overgeneralizations. Brief summaries of various definitions of transference are contained in Menninger's *Theory of Psychoanalytic Technique* (1961). For a thorough presentation of an interpersonal theory of behavior, consult Sullivan's *The Interpersonal Theory of Psychiatry* (1953). Horney's *Our Inner Conflicts* (1945) includes a detailed consideration of her ideas about the three modes of interpersonal relationships.

A complete exposition of the theory of defense mechanisms can be found in Munroe's *Schools of Psychoanalytic Thought* (1955). A somewhat different treatment of defense mechanisms is offered by Redl and Wineman in *The Aggressive Child* (1957). Freud's *The Ego and the Mechanisms of Defense* (1946) is a classic work in this area.

chapter 3

Joan

I

BACKGROUND INFORMATION

Intake Summary: November, 1962.

Identifying data. Joan has been referred to the institution by Children's Court, where she was brought by her father, who claimed she was unmanageable and incorrigible. She is 14½ years old and has one sister, age 9.

Family history. Joan is the older daughter of emotionally disturbed parents. Her father, who is in debt, earns a modest living as an operator in a woman's clothing manufacturing concern. He is a weak and passive individual who is dominated by his daughter as he was by his wife.

Her mother, a seriously disturbed woman, died from cancer a year ago after previous operations for the same disease. She had been an excellent ballet dancer and aspired to join the

American Ballet Theater. However, although the company offered her two auditions, she was too frightened to appear for them.

The father reported that the marriage was fraught with conflict and unhappiness because his wife was an unstable, immature, erratic woman. For this reason he had tried to spend as much time out of the house as possible. He had hoped that having a child would have a steadying influence upon his wife, but the children got on her nerves and she was very impatient with them. She seldom **spoke** to Joan; instead, she yelled at her, shook her by the hair, or abused her in other ways. When Joan showed an interest in dancing, her mother became very jealous and refused to take her to the school for lessons.

The father stated that although as a child Joan was very compliant, she became aggressive and defiant as she grew older. There was a long history of open hostility and conflict between her and her mother. They would yell at each other to "drop dead" and even hit each other. On one occasion Joan hit her mother on the breast and was subsequently blamed by an aunt for the death of her mother, who died of breast cancer.

Interview with father. The father reported that since the death of her mother, Joan had been keeping very late hours and had often sneaked into the apartment at two or three in the morning. On one occasion she stayed out all night, sleeping in a boy friend's hallway. She brought boys up to the apartment against her father's wishes while he was working. She refused to bathe and had run away repeatedly. She cursed him, used profane language, and intimidated him through temper tantrums and threats. He lost control of himself and hit her, even beating her once with a broomstick. He had tried to explain to Joan that because of her mother's death and her younger sister's inability to assume responsibility, she had to take care of the house and assume the responsibility for seeing to it that things ran smoothly. She, however, had been derelict in her duties. Her father also felt that Joan was sharp and abusive toward her sister and treated her in a manner similar to the way she herself had been treated by her mother. He thought that part of her problem was that she resented having to care for the house and her sister. He stated that Joan needed placement because she was unmanageable and may have a deleterious effect on the younger daughter if she remains at home.

Interview with Joan. Joan is a slim, 14½-year-old youngster. She uses cosmetics to extreme and has shaved her eyebrows and replaced them with grossly exaggerated penciled-in ones. She wears extremely tight-fitting dresses and low-cut blouses. Her general appearance is that of a dirty, sloppy, yet seductive youngster.

Joan talked readily about her problems. However, she had little insight into how she had contributed to them, tended to blame others for her difficulties, and complained about the way they had treated her. She stated that her father had brought her to Children's Court to punish her, not to help her. She said that he picked on her, called her a liar, complained about her poor housework, and told her that she was responsible for the house because her 9-year-old sister was too young. She reported that she had tried to take good care of the apartment, but her sister had been too messy and her father had expected her to do it all by herself. She complained bitterly that her father had told her that it would have been better if she rather than her mother had died.

She described her mother as a nervous and sick woman who had often become so angry that she had seemed on the verge of killing her. Nevertheless, she hated her father's family for the way they had treated her mother during the last few years.

The most obvious thing about this youngster was her extreme guilt. She blames herself for her mother's death and her father's debts and she apparently feels that by her bad behavior she had forced her father to go back on his promise to his wife to be both father and mother to their daughters.

Before she left the interview she said that she had no one to talk to now that her mother is gone. She felt very lonely and sad and seemed to be quite depressed.

Psychological Testing Prior to Admission

During most of the testing Joan was on the verge of tears because she was quite anxious and apprehensive about her capacities. She sought the examiner's reassurance and was able to profit from it.

At present Joan is overwhelmed by the predicament in which she finds herself. She is in conflict over whether to yield to her own adolescent impulses and fulfill her own often immature needs, or to behave in a more mature manner and devote herself to her family. At present her impulses have the upper hand. Although she has the potential for controlling her emotions and reacting appropriately to social situations on the basis of reason, she often reacts on the basis of her tempestuous emotional state. At these times she can be expected to be indiscriminate in her reactions. She will probably respond to very dissimilar situations in the same way because her response will be determined more by her emotional state than by the situation as it exists. On such occasions, her response would probably be characterized by inadequacy, helplessness, anger, and defiance.

Joan is an emotionally labile youngster given to periods of elation and depression. She feels quite alone and rejected and will probably attempt to attach herself to adults in a rather dependent manner.

At present she is suffering from feelings of extreme guilt related to her hostility toward her mother, her imagined role in her mother's death, and her inability to assume the burdens of the household. This guilt is a major factor in her conflict over whether to devote herself to her family or to follow her impulses. She seems to doubt that anyone would want to help her because she is such a "bad, worthless" girl. She is over-involved in receiving love, affection, and care from others, but she tends to anticipate. abuse and rejection. This anticipation interferes with her ability to establish meaningful relationships with others and leads her to read rejection even into acts of acceptance.

Joan has bright, normal intelligence. She graduated from a ninth-grade school, where she achieved at the ninth-grade level in reading and the 7.3-grade level in arithmetic. Thus, despite her emotional problems, her reading level is the proper one for her age. Her other academic skills appear to be well developed and relatively free from the disruptive influences of emotional problems. However, she is an angry and defiant youngster who will probably respond in these ways if under pressure. Although she is ready to continue high school work, her ability to do so will depend on her motivation and interest. With this in mind, it should be noted that despite her good school record she wishes to quit school and become a beautician or a dancer. She feels that the earnings from either career would enable her to buy clothes and things for herself and to avoid being a financial burden on her father.

Previous School Record

Her previous school reported that she had not been a behavior problem but had been sloppy in her appearance and a truant during her last school year.

SCHOOL GRADES PRIOR TO ADMITTANCE

	8A	8B	9A	9B
English	80	82	70	65
French	—	75	65	65
Math	70	80	65	65
Social Studies	80	90	75	65
Science	—	85	70	80
Health	85	75	85	90
Gym	80	75	90	90
Music	85	90	85	80
Fine Arts	80	—	79	68
Journalism	—	—	70	65

SECOND YEAR OF HIGH SCHOOL COMPLETED AT THE INSTITUTION

Initial Interview with Principal: December

Whenever we discussed what her problem had been in school, she kept referring to her parents, saying that those times when she had gone to school had not been fruitful because she had been so preoccupied with thoughts about her parents that she had been unable to concentrate on the work at hand. After I had handled her reluctance to return to school here, I explained to her what her school program would be like. She said that she would like to try schoolwork, but she was afraid that if she tried to do something and could not, she would break down and cry, or have a temper tantrum and destroy what she had done. I assured her that we understood such problems and would help her with them. At the end of the interview she doubted her ability to find her way around the campus and needed reassurance that she could get back to her cottage.

School Reports

During her sophomore year, Joan's school program emphasized nonacademic subjects. It included home economics, commercial subjects, English, and dancing lessons. Excerpts from her teachers' reports are included below.

Commercial Teacher (Mr. Kelly): January. Joan was a new student this period. She started out well and showed a positive attitude toward all aspects of the program. As of late, she has been in a tailspin. She cannot work and spends a great deal of her time trying to see her psychotherapist. She claims that she is very nervous and upset and that she cannot concentrate. She is generally very quiet and has little to do with the other students in the class. She sits in the back of the room and works by herself. When she is upset, she becomes extremely restless and politely asks for permission to leave class. If she does not receive permission to leave, she acts up as a way of forcing me to excuse her.

Homemaking Teacher (female): January. Joan is quiet and when in class tries to cooperate. She is not liked by the girls and stays to herself most of the time. She doesn't relate to her teacher and speaks very lów when spoken to. When she does not want to work, she just sits with her head buried. She does not have any initiative to learn or to be a part of the group. She has a very short interest span.

April. Although she is still quiet, she now comes in with a chip on her shoulder. She brought in two skirts to have zippers put in and to be fitted. When I told her she had to learn to operate the machine first, she became very indignant and said, "Why don't you fix them for me?" She often avoids the class. Even when she does come, she refuses to participate and just sits at my desk and annoys me. She is a below-average worker in both sewing and cooking. She must be told each step; otherwise, she gets lost and messes up her work. I have tried to help her with this. But when I ask her to tell me why she made the mistake, she replies: "I didn't know what to do. I had to do something, so I did anything." She wants me to think that she is too inept to do anything so that I will not expect anything from her.

Although she almost never talks to the girls, she has recently begun to relate more to me. For instance, she recently asked me if I would give her a ride into town the next time she has permission to go home for a visit.

English Teacher (male, not Mr. Williams): January. Initially Joan was a very quiet, withdrawn youngster who seldom participated in class. After a few months, her behavior changed. Now whenever I attempt to communicate with her she says, "Leave me alone. Mind your own business! Can't you see I'm upset?" Yet she complains that I ignore her. Her recent behavior during an examination was typical. She complained throughout that she did not know anything and demanded that I mark her paper immediately after she had completed it. When I refused, she wrenched the paper from my hand, ripped it in pieces, and threw it into the wastebasket, shouting, "I told you I couldn't do it." She is very sexy with me and I have had to ask her repeatedly to keep her hands off me. She spends most of her time in class waiting for the period to end and is apparently wasting her time in the classroom. She is capable of functioning well, but she does not realize this. Perhaps this is why she refuses to participate in class. Although she maintains that she wants to continue in the class, she might profit from a change in program.

Same teacher (from a note written to the principal): February. She ignores me completely and acts as if I have no authority over her. Her language is extremely abusive and foul. In addition, her class participation has decreased to the zero point. There seems to be little reason to continue her in the class.

From a memorandum from the principal regarding her dancing lessons. Joan behaved so seductively toward her teacher that her lessons were discontinued at his request.

Treatment Summaries

Initial psychiatric interview. Joan appears to be in a state of mourning for her mother. She shaved off her eyebrows shortly after her mother died and continues to wear black. She apparently has accepted many of her mother's punitive, rejecting, deprecating attitudes toward her into her own self-concept. However, at the same time, her mother's attitude has engendered violent, hateful, killing feelings in her about which she feels extremely guilty. Alone in her bed at night she is tortured and tormented by this guilt. She has become so frightened that she cannot sleep without a bright light in her room. Her dreams are terribly frightening. Often she sees herself in a coffin disappearing into nothingness. Sometimes her mother talks to her in her dreams. She says, "If you will be good, I will be proud of you." Then she feels guilty about the way she has behaved. At other times her mother says, "You killed me. I will kill you." Then she feels terrified.

During the interview she talked about her need to talk to a psychotherapist. She wanted one who would be devoted to her, not one who would be concerned with other things and people. She was very explicit about her preference for a male therapist. She felt a woman might get married or become pregnant and leave her. Or she might be too concerned with her own family to devote herself to one of her patients.

Psychotherapy reports: December to January. Joan's initial adjustment to cottage life was mixed. She adjusted well to the cottage parents and was compliant, cooperative, and adhered to the rules and regulations. However, she had great difficulty with the other girls, who subjected her to considerable hazing. This including "frenching" her bed, spilling depilatory lotion on her hair, and giving her "the silent treatment." She felt totally incapable of defending herself against this hazing and was afraid to tell the girls how she felt about it. At times she has been quite ingratiating with the girls in an attempt to curry favor with them, but to no avail.

She feels that she is missing a great deal in school because she is not as involved in academic work as she had been. Her goal is to return to the school she left and earn an academic diploma.

Joan's feelings toward her family are quite complex. She has become devoted to her mother's memory since her death and believes that her mother had been rejected and maligned by her family. She feels that she, too, has been rejected by them in that they have not assisted her financially despite their ability to do so. She also feels rejected by her father, whom she believes prefers her younger sister. Actually, she sees people in general as cold, disinterested, ungiving, and rejecting. She thinks of herself as a poor "Little Orphan Annie," and she is venting her anger against a world which she feels is treating her this way. She apparently provokes rejection and coldness in others. However, at present she is not aware of how she does this.

She has stated that she is nervous, moody, and high-strung like her mother. She also has numerous somatic and psychological complaints reminiscent of her mother's difficulties. She acts very demanding with me during our therapy sessions. She complains that I do not let her talk about whatever she wishes, reacts with anger and temper tantrums whenever her desires are not gratified immediately, and consistently accuses me of controlling her therapy sessions by choosing the topics for discussion.

Psychotherapy reports: February to June. Her cottage mother reported that she was totally inept and immature. She needed to be taught how to do her laundry, take care of her room, and so on. In view of the considerable responsibility she assumed at home for the household chores, it is difficult to understand her ineptness in the cottage. Perhaps this was a way of being dependent on her cottage mother or of gaining her attention.

Joan is constantly attempting to gain sympathy from the other girls. But she has little success because her constant complaints and reiterations of her previous difficulties merely alienate them. They see her not as a pathetic child, but as a nuisance. She has also tried, without success, to win their favor by lending things to them and doing favors for them. As a result her relationship with them is very frustrating. Periodically she becomes enraged at them either because she has catered too much to them or has held back too much of the anger she felt about the way they had treated her and yells and screams at them. However, she is too frightened of her hostility to follow through on her feelings. She blames her emotional disturbance rather than their actions for her anger and believes that she must have provoked them. At present she is an isolate and spends most of her time alone in her room.

In school her behavior has followed a consistent pattern. She began most class periods by being cooperative and interested. However, she soon became restless and asked to be excused to see another staff member. If this did not work, she claimed that she was upset and unable to concentrate, and demanded to be excused. Often she resorted to temper tantrums when all else failed. She alternated between two moods, excitation and depression. When she was excited and agitated her behavior was characterized by rage and temper tantrums. When she was depressed she cried, isolated herself from her peers, and clung to adults.

Joan was very adroit at convincing the staff members that she needed them. They responded to her requests for an understanding ear by making appointments to see her during class time, reducing demands on her, and commiserating with her about her "misfortunes." As a result, she was able to gain the attention she desired, but she also avoided too many of the tasks and too much of the responsibility expected of her. Staff members were informed of the meaning of her clinging, childlike behavior and they ceased responding in the manner described above. Now she finds it difficult to avoid class.

COMMENTS

1. What were Joan's major underlying problems?

The major problem underlying many of Joan's emotional difficulties was her inability to resolve one of the basic conflicts in the growing-up process. This was the conflict between her infantile wish for unconditional loving care and total immediate impulse gratification, and her belief that she should behave in more mature, socially responsible, and self-denying ways. Torn between these two alternative sources of satisfaction, she was unable to obtain satisfaction through either one. She was unable to find it through gratifying her impulses or seeking unconditional love because she was much too old to be allowed to yield to her impulses or to be given the unconditional care only infants receive. In addition, because of her conflict, seeking impulse gratification and unconditional loving care made her feel too guilty about not behaving in more socially responsible and self-denying ways to be comfortable with such behavior.

Her attempts to achieve satisfaction by behaving in more socially responsible, self-denying ways were equally abortive because they made her feel angry about sacrificing her own desires and fearful that she was succumbing to the control of others. Ever aware of her unmet desires, frustrated in her attempts to satisfy them, and bombarded by the discomforting emotions produced by her conflict, she remained an extremely depressed and anxious youngster.

2. Which defense mechanisms and interpersonal techniques did she employ to cope with the emotional problems associated with her unresolved conflict?

Joan's basic way of dealing with her emotional problems was to move toward people. Her initial relationships with others were characterized by conformity, ingratiation, self-sacrifice, helplessness, and inadequacy. In this way she attempted to win the affection, loving care, and permission for infantile impulse gratification which was necessary to assuage her anxiety and depression. This approach usually met with some initial success. However, in time, her constant complaints usually alienated others and her demands for assistance, affection, and impulse gratification became too excessive to be tolerated by others. Moreover, she herself soon became too resentful of the temporary delay in impulse gratification and too fearful of the loss of personal integrity which her ingratiating, conforming behavior necessitated to continue behaving this way. Since she was unable to continue to obtain satisfaction by moving toward others, the depression and anxiety she had previously assuaged in this manner threatened her once again.

She was able to erect a temporary barrier against the reinstatement of these discomforting emotions through defensive misperceptions and reaction formations. When the staff denied her infantile wishes she defended herself against the belief that she warranted their rejection because of her own unreasonableness by misperceiving the staff as unreasonably mean and rejecting. This enabled her to feel angry toward them as a reaction formation against the depression she might otherwise have felt. But she was unable to sustain this defense because her self-deprecating attitude was too intense to be submerged by the misperception and her guilt about hostility was too strong to allow her to continue to move against others.

With the reinstatement of her depression, despite her movement toward and against others, she moved away from them. However, since this only added loneliness and isolation to her depression and anxiety, she once again reached out toward others in an even more desperate bid for the unconditional loving care she needed to dispel her pain. This completed the cycle, added another group of failures to the many she had already experienced, and renewed the conflict once again.

3. What kinds of educational difficulties might result from her emotional problems?

Her educational functioning would probably vary with her emotional state. When she felt helpless, inadequate, and anxious she might try to avoid any educational challenges. When she felt depressed she would probably be unable to succeed even if she were able to attempt to do so. Since her emotional upsets occurred in cycles, her educational difficulties would probably do so as well.

Her relationships with her teachers would tend to be affected by these same cycles. Of course, the educator's own actions would have some influence on Joan's reaction to him. But it is likely that her emotional state would exert a greater influence upon whether she would move toward, against, or away from him.

4. What factors should an educator consider in attempting to deal with these problems?

In order to encourage Joan to resolve her conflict in favor of more mature and socially desirable classroom behavior, the educator must not only enhance the outcome of such behavior but also deal with the resentment and anger likely to develop because of the delay in impulse gratification and her perceived succumbing to external control that such behavior necessitates.

Since Joan acted in a helpless, inadequate manner when she was anxious about her ability to succeed as well as when she wanted to induce others to give her additional loving care, the educator must determine whether she actually is anxious about a specific task when she responds helplessly to it or is only using the situation as an opportunity to obtain some more loving care.

When confronted by her disruptive behavior he must determine whether it is behavior she cannot control or a more controllable "last resort" attempt to intimidate him. The same spirit of inquiry should be applied to her statements that she is too upset to work.

II

SECOND YEAR AT THE INSTITUTION

School Reports

Joan's program consisted of the following subjects: world history, English III, biology, commercial subjects.

Biology teacher (Mr. Roth), initial report: January.   At the beginning of the term Joan was attentive, cooperative, and motivated. She seemed to be genuinely interested in the work. However, by the end of September she seemed to be exploiting the class and the teacher. It was as if she had been spending the first few weeks developing a good relationship with me which could be exploited at a later date. She began to act as if I were her medical adviser. Three or four times a week she would ask me to treat minor lacerations on her hands, arms, or back. After a few weeks I began to tell her to see the nurse about them. When I did this she stopped having accidental injuries for me to treat.

Joan constantly chews and cracks gum in class in order to get a reaction from me. I told her quite often that although I realized that she might need to chew gum, I could not accept the cracking that went along with it. I told her that I had gone halfway by allowing her to chew gum in class and asked her to meet me halfway by not cracking the gum.

I believe that Joan needs structure. This is especially necessary when she refuses to listen to my requests that she start working, open a book, take an examination, and so on. She needs direction and firmness tempered by understanding. Therefore, on these occasions I demand that she work, place a pencil in her hand, open her book for her, and tell her that if she does not begin working I will send her to the principal.

Joan has a great many self-doubts. She is constantly asking me questions about heredity, mental illness, amnesia, and various diseases. She appears to be quite worried about this. During one class period, when we were discussing cancer, she began to cry. Suddenly she was screaming and demanding that I stop the discussion. I explained to her why I could not do this and suggested that she stay outside until she had regained control of herself. She left but returned shortly before the end of the period and explained that her mother had died from cancer. Since then she has never displayed such outbursts when the topic has been discussed.

Biology is probably difficult for Joan because many of the topics upset her. When we begin such a topic, she refuses to attend to the subject matter. This is especially true when we are studying the nervous system. She uses these occasions as excuses for becoming disturbed. Her friend Deborah does the same thing and then they both use it as an opportunity to goof off and ruin the period.

Sometimes the work in class is too difficult for her. This is usually when we are starting a new topic. At these times she becomes agitated, claims that she does not understand the work, and gives up attempting to succeed. When this happens I point out to her that it is normal for anyone, including her, to be apprehensive about work that is new and I try to encourage her to overcome her apprehensiveness. In order to build up her self-confidence, I point out her successes in previous units which were just as difficult for her at first. In fact, I have continually complimented her wherever possible about a nice dress or a new hair-do in order to help her feel better about herself.

Joan often compares herself to Deborah, whom she thinks is the incarnation of perfection. This, of course, adds to her self-doubts because she is not as good a student as Deborah is. She also joins in whenever Deborah behaves disruptively.

Joan wants sympathy from adults. She complained to me that the staff members laugh at her when she tells them about her problems and that all she wants is to be helped to lead a normal life. She believes that no one cares for her because most of the people whom she has loved and trusted have left her. When she feels this way during class she is extremely melancholy and apathetic. Recently she became hysterical in class when someone whispered to her that her boy friend had just been sent to a state mental hospital. She ran out of the room screaming, crying, and threatening to push her hand through a window and thus take her own life. I tried to calm her by pointing out to her all the things that she had to live for. I explained that there were people less fortunate than she — people with physical handicaps which could never be corrected while she was already overcoming her handicaps through the insight she has gained about herself and others. She stopped crying, thought a while, and came back into the class. Later, at my suggestion, she discussed the incident with the principal.

I feel that Joan can certainly be helped. She needs even more acceptance, help, care, and attention than she has been receiving. Unfortunately, Joan has learned that those who make the most noise and cause the greatest disturbance often receive the most attention. This is probably a major reason for her recent outbursts. This is especially bad for her because it does not help her learn self-control. Joan mentioned that although she needs to continue her dancing lessons and has been asking to have them again, they have not been continued. Recently she said to me that she will soon be forced to lose interest in dancing — the thing she likes best. This would be a very unfortunate occurrence and should be avoided.

Report card comment. Joan is doing well. With a little more effort she could earn an even better grade.

Spring report (the class was now coeducational). At the beginning of the second term Joan attempted to do her work and control her behavior. She attended class and completed most of her assignments. Recently events which have occurred in her cottage and in psychotherapy sessions have interfered with her classroom functioning because she brings all her difficulties into the classroom with her. For example, today she was upset that she had not allowed to stay up late in order to watch television the night before. She refused to work, tore papers, broke pencils, paced the floor, stared out of the window, and screamed, "Leave me alone!" when I asked her to sit down.

The other day she walked into the classroom and sat in the back of the room instead of in her own seat. I knew that she had seen her therapist earlier in the day and was disheartened by the conference. However, I also knew that we must not continue to allow her to withdraw into herself and not function. Hoping to involve her in the work, I asked her if she had a pencil. She said that she was not going to do any work and did not need one. I told her that if she did not want to work in the class she would have to sit in the principal's office. She refused to work and I placed her name on the misbehavior list. She stated that she was not going to work or to leave the room. After I had spent five minutes of the class time attempting to reason with her, I had to walk up to her and gradually nudge her to the door. She began to scream, curse, and threaten me. Then I told her and the class that the term was drawing to a close and we no longer could afford to devote class time to her disruptions. I stated very strongly to her and the rest of the class that I would not surrender to her demands just because she was persistent in them. I also let her know that she had better begin to help herself because if she did not make an attempt to improve her habits, she would not pass the course.

Final report: June.   Joan has made a tremendous amount of progress during the past three months. Her study habits have improved immensely. Now she is able to read through the chapter before she asks questions about the work. She has been able to control her behavior even when emotionally upset. Although she is still somewhat disturbed by discussions of disease, she no longer loses control of herself. In the past few weeks I have heard her compliment her peers, giving them recognition for their accomplishments. This also is a very positive area for her. I have noticed that she no longer looks up to Deborah, whom she thought was completely perfect and therefore vastly superior to her. She not only acts less disturbed but looks the part. For the past month or so she has dressed conservatively, using her makeup with extreme reservation.

Biology was a difficult and challenging subject for her. She tried her best to succeed and in doing so she has become confident that she can succeed academically. She has also learned to relate to her peers. I believe that she has made a tremendous change for the better. I am confident that now she could succeed in a regular high school.

Report card comment.   Congratulations for your fine, sometimes excellent work.

From a note written to the principal.   Joan should receive a commendation for her excellent improvement. I am sure this has increased her self-assurance tremendously.

Social Studies and English Teacher (Mr. Williams)

Initial report: November. Joan was an academic failure during the first six weeks of the term. She lacked confidence in her ability, did not complete her homework assignments, and refused to take any examinations. Her functioning has improved during the last few weeks. Her self-confidence is growing, she has completed most of her homework, and she has taken many of the spelling examinations which she had missed. She used to think that "something was wrong with her mind" because she was unable to remember "anything." Now she is ecstatic because she can remember things which we had discussed in previous classes.

A while ago after she had completed a spelling test she suddenly rose from her seat, ripped up the paper, and threw it into the wastepaper basket. After class I collected the pieces and put them together. When she returned to class the next day I showed her how well she had done. This was quite a surprise to her. Later, in fact two weeks ago, she refused to hand in another spelling paper. This time I insisted that she do so because I thought she had learned her lesson from the previous incident. Instead of giving me the paper she ran screaming to her therapist. I followed her there at the end of the period. After a three-way discussion Joan agreed to give me her paper. This time it was quite poor because she had not studied.

Last week she thought that I had marked one of her history examinations too strictly. I looked at it with her and explained why her grade was correct. She argued for awhile and then ran out of the room, screaming that I was unfair. She returned the next period and coyly asked me if I could substitute another question because she had misunderstood the one which she had claimed that I had marked too strictly. She had never been so cooperative before.

Joan has a strong desire to have everything her own way. Until recently she used to ask me to do things which I could not do. When I refused, she screamed, threatened, cursed, and swore that she hated me. When these outbursts did not make me angry she became infuriated and acted up even more. She has not behaved this way for the last two weeks. She still tells me that she hates me, but now she does so in a playful manner but still without any apparent reason.

Her work has improved considerably. However, she is more interested in proving to herself that she can do well than she is in understanding the subject matter.

Report card comment. Joan has expended a great deal of effort trying to improve herself. The results of her efforts are quite obvious.

April (the class has become coeducational). Joan is functioning much better in class. She takes all her examinations, accepts some criticism, and completes all her work. However, she is still quite anxious about her work and her study habits are still poor. She tries to memorize rather than understand textbook material, misinterprets questions, and lacks the ability to concentrate on one thing for any length of time.

She enjoys and encourages the attention of the boys in the class but relates to them in a childlike manner. She hits and slaps them in a playful manner and then becomes angry when they retaliate in kind. Although I have tried to point it out to her, she seems to be unaware that she brings the difficulties on herself.

Joan often comes to class moody. When she is in a bad mood she gets angry with me if I smile at anyone and when she is unprepared she becomes angry at others because they supposedly "prevent" her from learning. I have told her that these requests that I stop smiling and that the students stop interfering with her learning are inappropriate.

She is very negativistic; her immediate response to anything is "no." She often prefaces a remark with "No" even though it makes no sense in context. I have found that ignoring her initial "No" is the best procedure because it usually does not reflect her actual feelings. In spite of these problems, because of the fine progress she has made, she might be ready to attend a normal public school this summer. I believe that it would be a real gamble but it could work out well.

June. Joan's functioning has continued to improve. During the past few months she handed in all her assignments, participated more actively in class, exhibited more self-assurance, and was better able to accept constructive criticism. Before this she competed with the other students in the class, especially Deborah, in terms of grades. Now she claims that she is willing to accept whatever grade she earns because she knows that she has tried her best. Even her personal appearance has improved.

She still has a number of problems. She hesitates to answer questions in class because, as she put it, she is afraid of making a mistake, especially in front of the boys. This indicates that she lacks sufficient confidence in her abilities. She tries to manipulate me to give her the things she wants by continuously requesting them and disrupting the class when I refuse.

In spite of these problems she has done well. She earned the privilege of going off-grounds to school by her hard work.

Report card comment.   Congratulations on your fine progress. You had to overcome many problems to do as well as you have done.

Commercial Teacher (Mr. Kelly)

Initial report: November.   Joan functions rather erratically. At times, she settles down and works well, particularly in her business practice. In this subject she sets a good standard for herself, functions at the upper level of her class, follows through on her assignments, and shows an interest in the results of her work. Typing which is a more demanding subject has been a problem for her. She has shown very little aptitude in this subject. She often gets discouraged, throws up her hands in frustration, fails to see purpose in her work, and stops.

She relates well to the teacher and usually responds well to him. However, on those days when she is upset, little can be accomplished with her. She becomes very depressed, negativistic, restless, and provocative. This often occurs when she is upset about something which has not happened in this class.

Spring.   Joan quieted down this period. She had fewer

emotional upsets, worked more consistently, and showed more interest in her work. Although she did not gravitate toward any particular girl, she communicated with most of them and felt comfortable in the group. She was more able to stay in class and her personal appearance improved.

Final report: June. Joan has always had poor aptitude for typing and could therefore make little progress in this subject. This caused a great deal of frustration for her and affected her interest in other subjects of the course.

It had always been difficult for her to accept the fact that she just did not have a great deal of aptitude for typing. During this final period she finally accepted this and asked for a modified program. She spent most of her class time working on her business practices, in which she did good work, and typing her biology notes. Joan has shown considerable improvement in her general appearance, behavior, and attitude during the last quarter. She has remained in the program with less effort and has not presented any management problems. She got along well with the other students and related well to the teacher. She worked at the top level of her class in business practice and was able to set good standards for herself in this subject. She would follow through on her assignments and took particular interest in the grades she received. Even before she completed the entire assignment, she would have me grade the first half of it because, as she would say, "I want to see if I am doing it right." This was the only aspect of the course in which she showed an interest. Although she learned to run the different office machines, she would not follow through to develop her skills.

Grades

	STATE-WIDE EXAMINATION	FINAL GRADE
English	65	75
World History	80	80
Biology	72	75
Business Practices		80
Typing		75

Report of Vocational Evaluation: May

Joan's expressed pattern of interest seems to be borne out by the interest inventory. Although she did not show a strong preference for business activity, it was nonetheless a positive area in the tests. Her interest actually divides itself between dancing and music, and clerical activities. In the clerical areas, she has good aptitude for various types of clerical training including stenography and appears to have good abilities to handle people and situations in sales or public relations work. It was not possible to test for dancing ability, but this is such a strong area of interest for her that an evaluation of aptitude in this area seems indicated.

The test results indicate quite clearly that she has the necessary intellectual abilities and organizational skills to complete high school. According to her pattern of interests, however, she might prefer to take an academic course with a music rather than a commercial major. She has the intellectual capacity for this, but a question would have to be raised about her emotional readiness to undertake this type of training on a consistent basis. On the other hand, if she chooses a commercial course which she might be able to complete easily, she might also take a music major with it and perhaps do quite well in both areas. Specific recommendations based on the test results are:

1. She is psychologically and academically ready for high school work and should be encouraged to continue her academic work on grounds. This is a child who will eventually be able to go off-grounds to attend school.

2. She has good clerical aptitudes and good abilities in handling people in various types of situations. Therefore, commercial training, preferably along clerical and secretarial lines, is suggested. This could be done, if at all possible, as part of her high school training, but not as specific additional training until she is ready for it.

3. Her interest in music and dancing is so intense that she should be evaluated. Since such training is rigorous and long,

this might be a constant goal toward which she could work while earning a living in a more practicable way.

Psychotherapy Summaries (new therapist): September to October. Joan had little control over herself during this period. It was difficult for her to remain in class and she often convinced her teachers to allow her to see me because she stated she was "too upset to work." However, instead of meeting me, she spent most of her out-of-class time wandering around the buildings or talking with boys. She gave many staff members the impression that she was an extremely abandoned child who needed to talk to them. Many of them felt that they had been singled out as the only person to whom she could talk. As a result of my intervention they were able to see the true nature of her behavior. Now they set more limits and expect more from her.

She had trouble throughout the institution around the time of her sixteenth birthday. She demanded extra privileges from people as a kind of birthday present. When they refused because of the unrealistic nature of her requests, she reacted as if she had been rejected and abandoned.

In school she was exhilarated by success but overwhelmed by failure. When she was anxious in class she misperceived her teachers as threatening and rejecting. In our sessions, I am trying to help her see how she misperceives hostility and rejection and also how she provokes them by her incessant complaints and unreasonable demands.

She seems to be involved in a cycle in which she demands more privileges, attention, and solicitude than others can give, feels rejected by them when they do not gratify her, and reacts with sarcasm and hostility. Hopefully an increase in the amount of success she experiences in school and elsewhere can cut into this cycle. Increased success could lead to a decrease in her demands and complaints, which would evoke less rejection and retaliation from others, and, in turn, less hostility from her.

I am also trying to help her become more oriented to the real world about her. This would enable her to meet with more success and it would attract her from the world of fantasy which absorbs so much of her interest.

November to December.   She is improving in all areas. In the cottage she is more relaxed and gets along better with the other girls. She can now comply with her cottage parents' requests without first rebelling, or without behaving so submissively that she is later enraged at her own passivity.

She has shown tremendous improvement in school, perhaps because she has met with more success than she expected. As a result she has a strong desire to finish high school. Now she sees how she demanded too much and used her illness to avoid work and tests. Recently she asked me to arrange a meeting with the principal in order to discuss ways in which her teachers could help her conform to the school structure. She wanted this because it would help her adjust to a normal school in the future.

Although she has made these advances, she still feels anxious, rejected, and left out in groups. Although she no longer dresses or talks as if she were in mourning for her mother, she continues to dress and use cosmetics in an unflattering manner. She still maintains a dependent relationship with other girls, who tell her how to make up, help her dress, and choose her clothes.

I have increasingly pointed out to her how she has tried to provoke me into acting angrily. She still does not see how she misperceives that I control her therapy sessions.

January to April.   Joan is beginning to see how her provocative behavior not only angers others but also keeps them at a distance and prevents her from developing close relationships with them. Perhaps she acts this way because she feels that she will lose anyone toward whom she feels close and is defending herself against this loss.

June.   She was unusually eager to start the discussion. She stated that she felt she had gotten everything she ever wanted from others by shouting, crying, and throwing temper tantrums, and she expressed her awareness that this made her feel guilty whenever she got what she wanted.

COMMENTS

1. What kinds of educational problems resulted from each of the following?

Her infantile desires for immediate impulse gratification and unconditional loving care

Her fear of succumbing to external control

Her depression and anger

Her anxiety about her perceived helplessness and inadequacy.

Joan's infantile desires for immediate impulse gratification and unconditional loving care made it difficult for her to accept the frustrations and delays in gratification necessary for gradual educational progress. Her infantile desires also interfered with her ability to maintain close relationships with her teachers because they led her to make requests of them which they could not fulfill.

Her fear of succumbing to external control also limited her ability to maintain a close relationship with her teachers. In addition, it contributed to her initially negative response to many of the expectations and demands they placed upon her.

Her depression and anger prevented her from attending to the work in progress. On occasion they also help lead her to behave in ways which disrupted the class and strained her relationships with her teachers.

Her anxiety about her perceived helplessness and inadequacy in the face of educational tasks led her to avoid new topics and examinations and helped to make her hesitant about answering in class. Her anxieties about herself also decreased her tolerance for some aspects of the biology curriculum.

2. How might the educator deal with the following problems?

Her avoidance of educational challenge. The first task facing the educator is to reduce her anxiety to the point that she can meet the challenge she prefers to avoid. One of the most efficient techniques for assuaging her anxiety is to temper her unrealistic fears of failure with doses of reality. For example, when she is anxious about a new topic, the educator can assure her, as Mr. Roth did, that some anxiety is a normal and desirable thing, remind her that she has succeeded in tasks about which she had been initially anxious, and point out to her that she has the skills necessary for a successful performance of the task.

Another technique for assuaging her anxiety is to de-emphasize any evaluations of her work. This can be done in many ways. The educator can inform her that he considers her initial attempts to master a new topic as learning experience, not occasions for evaluation. He can assure her that any evaluation of her mastery of the topic will occur only after she has had sufficient opportunities to learn it. He can even suggest that she think of her initial attempt more as an exercise in facing her anxieties about new topics than an initial attempt to master a topic. Finally, he can also assure her that her achievements will be evaluated not in terms of what the other students accomplish, but in terms of her own capacities. This last measure could be particularly important because of Joan's tendency to compare herself unfavorably with others.

A third technique for increasing her confidence in her educational taskability is to build up her general confidence. Any contribution the educator can make toward the improvement of her overall self-concept would have its effect on her educational functioning. Treating her with dignity and respect, noting when she is dressed particularly attractively, and giving her as much realistic praise and recognition as possible would be especially desirable. In the long run, the success of the educator's efforts to assuage her anxiety about new topics and examinations will depend on her own success in these efforts. If she fails after he has encouraged her to try, she will be less likely to try again. If she succeeds, his encouragement could become unnecessary.

Unfortunately, as Mr. Williams discovered, it is probable

that Joan's emotional problems will occasionally cause her to fail despite all the educator's efforts to the contrary. When reversal occurs, the educator must be prepared to mitigate their effects. Again, reality testing is his best ally.

Through such reality testing devices as pointing out to her that she passed her spelling test when she studied, and that she failed when she did not, the educator can help her avoid the error of mistakenly attributing her failures to an imagined lack of ability or a defect in her "mind" when they are actually due to transitory lapses of effort or concentration.

Encouraging her to attempt to succeed in spite of her fears of failure, ensuring that her attempts to succeed will be fruitful, and mitigating the effects of occasional failures should do much to increase her confidence in her taskability. However, there may be occasions, especially early in the term before the educator's efforts have borne their fruits, when she will be too anxious to meet a particular educational challenge. On such occasions, postponing the confrontation and providing her with another opportunity to meet the challenge when she is less anxious, may contribute to a later success. This, in turn, would lessen her need for such postponements.

If because of her anxiety the educator chooses to make these temporary adjustments in his demands, he should guard against two dangers. First, she may come to rely on these postponements as crutches. He might explain to her that although they are temporarily expedient, they will be decreased as the necessity for them diminishes because they are undesirable in the long run. Reminding her that she must eventually learn to readjust to a normal school might also be helpful. Second, he should guard against encouraging her use of inappropriate techniques for obtaining postponements. He could inform her that he is making the adjustments because they are necessary and not because of the temper tantrums or because of any feminine wiles she might have employed in her attempts to achieve them. He could also suggest that she use other more desirable techniques for communicating her needs to him. Anticipating her need for adjustment would be the most effective way to avoid encouraging her use of inappropriate techniques for obtaining them.

Her emotional reaction to some of the more threatening aspects of the biology curriculum.   Her reaction to the discussion of disease in the biology class, like her avoidance of educational challenges, was the result of anxiety. However, her reaction to the discussion of disease, unlike her reaction to challenging tasks, resulted from hypochondria rather than from fears of inadequacy. The hypochondriacal concerns require a psychotherapeutic rather than an educational solution. However, the educator can help the situation by reassuringly communicating his understanding of her feelings and encouraging her to explore them with her therapist. Providing her with another opportunity to study the topic when she is more able to do so would be helpful educationally. It might also allay her discomfort about being unable to participate initially when asked to do so. This would be particularly appropriate for her reaction to discussions of cancer in which guilt about her imagined role in her mother's death probably compounded her hypochondriacal concerns. The earlier words of caution about discouraging her from either using her difficulties as an excuse to avoid educational tasks or learning to use inappropriate techniques for attaining her desires, would apply to these compromises as well. They would also apply to the others suggested below.

Her negative reactions to many of the demands and expectations placed on her.   This discussion is concerned with her negative reactions which were primarily a response to a fear of external control. Those which were due to other factors, such as concern about inadequacy or feelings of depression, are considered in other sections.

Since many of her negative reactions reflected a relatively flexible initial response to a demand rather than a deep-seated intransigent one, the educator's own initial response to her negativism might be to ignore it. Ignoring her negativism and continuing as if it had not been expressed, as Mr. Williams did, might make it possible to capture her by means of the intrinsic challenge or interest of the matter at hand. Responding to it, on the other hand, could easily create an issue where none had existed previously.

When her initial "No" cannot be overcome by ignoring it, it might be turned aside by removing the demand against which she is rebelling. Changing a demand which carries an obligation to a request which does not may assuage enough of her fear of external control to enable her more positive motivation to do its work without interference. This technique should be used sparingly lest it encourage her negativism by rewarding it.

When the structure of the class, the school policies, or the realities of the situation require conformity, the educator may not be able to gamble that Joan would choose to conform if she were given the privilege not to do so. In such cases, taking the extra time to explain why she must conform could lessen both her reluctance to do so and the possibility of hostile transference. Stating his awareness that his actions could be misconstrued as an attempt to inflict his will upon her as well as assuring her that this is not the case could also help.

Whether the educator elects to ignore her negativism, to afford her a choice, or to insist that she conform despite it, it would probably be beneficial to point out to her the self-defeating aspect of her negativism and to encourage her to discuss it with her therapist. In addition, the educator might ask himself whether he had inadvertently done anything which exacerbated her fear of external control. For although her negativism may be merely a specific instance of a period of general negativism to the demands of her environment, or an unjustified fear of being controlled by him, it could also be related to specific events in the classroom, such as his use of her positive feelings for him to encourage her to do things to please him.

Her requests for loving care. Since whatever else they were, her demands for unconditional loving care were all attempts to assuage her depressing feelings of undesirability and rejection; hence they should all be treated as such, regardless of the different forms in which they were put. As expressions of a desire for love, they should not summarily be dismissed as nuisances designed to bother the educator even if they are extremely bothersome. As undesirable results of her troubled feelings, they should not be considered inappropriate even though they are inappropriate to the external situation. They should be dealt with as any request for love would be dealt with: fulfilled if possible and, if not, denied with an adequate explanation.

The educator's decision whether to satisfy a specific request would depend on many things. One of these would be her therapist's opinion about whether fulfilling her request would either provide her with an unnecessary crutch or serve an undesirable additional purpose. An excellent example of this was her therapist's intervention when staff members were furthering her efforts to avoid class.

Different classroom structures and school policies would dictate varying reactions to the requests she made of her teachers. The structure and policy of Joan's class and school suggest the following reactions to some of her requests described in the anecdotal material. Her requests, either implicit or explicit, for intervention on the part of other staff members on behalf of her wish to have her dancing lessons reinstated would not be fulfilled. Instead she would be encouraged to reopen the question with the appropriate staff member. Her requests for first-aid treatment would be denied because a biology teacher is not as qualified to administer these services as a medically trained person. Her requests for special favors, such as rides home, might be fulfilled if and only if her therapist agreed. Her request of the homemaking teacher that she sew her skirts for her has educational implications because it involves a request for permission to avoid a learning situation. For this reason her request would be denied with the explanation that the teacher's job is to help her to learn how to do things for herself. Instead of sewing both skirts, the teacher might sew one for her while demonstrating how it is done and ask her to sew the other one herself when she had learned how to do it.

Her seductiveness and profanity. Her seductiveness and profanity, in and of themselves, did not interfere with her academic problems, but her teachers' discomfort about her behavior interfered in their relationships with her. If the educator's discomfort is the sole reason for his attempts to change her behavior, it might be better if he were to deal with his discomfort in supervision and not involve Joan at all. On the other hand, he may consider all inappropriate, disturbed behavior as an educational problem. If so, his main function in the total approach to her behavior would be to make her aware that her behavior is inappropriate for the classroom and especially inappropriate between a fifteen-year-old youngster and an adult educator and to encourage her to discuss it with her therapist.

Her inability to function adequately when beset by strong emotions. When Joan claims to be "too upset to work" or wants the teacher to "leave her alone," the educator's first task is to determine whether in fact she is too angry, depressed, or preoccupied by her thoughts to attend to the work at hand. For she may be able to become involved in the work despite her feelings, either because of its intrinsic interest and challenge or because of the escape it offers from her uncomfortable preoccupations.

There are many clues which the educator can use to determine whether Joan is actually too upset to work. He may be aware of any events in the immediate past, such as a recent session with her therapist, a home visit, or an argument in the previous class which was upsetting enough to prevent her from working. He can gain some empathic feeling about her emotional state through observing her dress, grooming, expression, and general demeanor. Finally, he might make an initial attempt to draw her into the mainstream of the class while noting her response.

If the evidence suggests that she is unable to attend, the educator would risk provoking her anger, defiance, and fear of control if he were to insist that she do so. Providing her with another activity to which she could relate would be one desirable alternative. Allowing her to remain in class without participating or excusing her to an area set aside for youngsters who are upset is another possibility. Punishing her for not participating in the hope of increasing her motivation to do so does not appear to be a desirable alternative in this case. Punishment would not mitigate the depression or anger which precluded her participation. On the contrary, it might exacerbate these feelings because of its connotation that she had done something "bad" or "wrong" for which she should be punished.

Disruptive Behavior

The measures suggested above for dealing with the problems which were created by Joan's infantile desires, fear of succumbing to external controls, feelings of inadequacy, and discomforting emotions should eliminate many of the causes of her disruptive behavior. If occasional outbursts occur despite these measures, the educator must decide whether to tolerate them in class until they have run their course or excuse her until she is ready to return. These alternatives have their advantages and disadvantages. Within the structure of her school, Joan would probably be asked to leave the class in order not to impede the progress of the other students. When it becomes necessary for the educator to ask her to leave, in the light of her fears of rejection and control it would probably be helpful to explain to her that he is not asking her to leave because he is unaware of her problems, or because he does not want to discuss them with her, or because he wants to punish her, but because he must continue the lesson for the sake of the other students. If she refuses to leave, as she did in the biology class, it would be better for the teacher to avoid any physical involvement with her by asking another staff member to escort her out of the room.

These suggestions are made with the aim of **impersonalizing** the interaction with her as much as possible so that the educator's actions are seen as the result of the situation and not the result of his personal feelings about her. The educator may not achieve this objective. Joan may be unable to perceive his actions accurately because of her emotional problems. He may be so emotionally involved in the problem that his actions do reflect his feelings at the moment. However, if his goal is attained, it may protect his relationship with her from being unnecessarily harmed by one unfortunate incident.

3. How appropriate were Mr. Roth's and Mr. William's attempts to deal with these problems?

Mr. Roth. Mr. Roth was quite aware of Joan's feelings of inadequacy and rejection. He consistently attempted to build up her self-confidence through complimentary comments, realistic praise, and reality testing. He was less consistent in his reaction to her disruptive behavior and her inability to function when she was emotionally upset. This inconsistency seems to have stemmed from two sources. The first was his inability to assess her powers of self-control. This difficulty is revealed in the conflict between his statement that she was upset by discussions of disease and his belief that she used these occasions as excuses to "goof off." The second source of his inconsistency was his occasional readiness to assume that some of the things she did in order to assuage her disturbing emotions were done to provoke him or to win a power struggle with him. His beliefs that she had developed a good relationship with him in order to exploit it, his conviction that she often did things in order to obtain a reaction from him, and his negative comments about her in front of her peers are indicative of this tendency.

These two characteristics help to explain why on some occasions, for example, when she was anxious about a new topic or was upset by an occurrence in the classroom, such as a discussion of cancer or news about the transfer of her boyfriend, he was reassuring, understanding, and permissive. But on other occasions, apparently those in which the disturbing event had occurred prior to her entrance into the class, he insisted that she function, threatened her with punishments if she did not, and battled with her in front of the class when she refused to comply.

Mr. Williams. Mr. Williams, like Mr. Roth, was aware of her feelings of inadequacy. He, too, used praise and reality testing to help her change her self-concept. However, his way of dealing with many of her other problems was different. He did not tend to personalize her actions or even her threats and curses; he was less likely to fulfill her requests, he was more likely to ignore an initial "No," and perhaps less likely to offer her reassurance and understanding. In general, his basic approach to her difficulties was to ignore them until they forced him to react and to impersonalize his actions when they did. This seems to have worked well in most instances. However, his tendency to ignore her difficulties seemed to have led him to recommend that she be sent off grounds to school, not because she was ready but because she had "earned the privilege" of going.

4. Joan's teachers believed that she was ready to attend an "off-grounds" school at the end of the school year. Was she ready to do so?

Although Joan was able to pass all her subjects in June, she still had not solved many of her educational problems. Moreover, the important improvements in her classroom behavior had taken place quite recently, many only within the previous two months.

The change from the protective, structured environment of the institution's school to the demanding and less controlled normal school situation might be too much for her to handle in spite of her recent progress. It might be threatening enough to cause her to revert to her earlier behavior patterns.

The importance of a successful experience in a normal classroom situation at this time when her self-concept and behavior were in a state of flux cannot be overvalued. However, for just this same reason an experience of failing could be devastating.

She still has a number of difficulties in her classroom functioning, and her changed self-concept and self-acceptance, not having had a chance to be reinforced, are still probably tentative; hence the prognosis for a successful experience in a normal school situation is guarded. Therefore, the change should be delayed. At the very least, her ability to succeed in a normal school should be tested by her ability to succeed in a normal summer school program. Furthermore, a successful experience during the summer might give her the extra confidence requisite for success during the regular academic year.

RECOMMENDED READINGS

For an analyses of the way conflicting motivation affects behavior see Dollard and Miller, *Personality and Psychotherapy* (1950). Rogers discusses the self-concept at length in his *Client-Centered Therapy* (1951).

Freud's *The Problem of Anxiety* (1936) contains an incisive consideration of the relationships between anxiety and personality in terms of psychoanalytic theory. May's *The Meaning of Anxiety* (1950) offers a somewhat different approach to the understanding of the effects of anxiety. *The Gambler* (originally published in 1866) by Dostoevsky is a marvelous characterization of the person in conflict. His *Notes from the Underground* (1864) describe the self-deprecating person in all of his despair and anguish.

chapter 4

Deborah

I

BACKGROUND INFORMATION

Intake Summary: March, 1962.

Family history. Deborah, age 14, is the oldest of four children of a middle-class family. Little is known about her early childhood. Her relationship with her mother was very strained until the mother died five years ago. Her father, who blames Deborah for her mother's death, stated that she had always been stubborn, defiant, and uncooperative with her mother. He is quite inconsistent in his relationship with her. On numerous occasions he has danced with her to rock-and-roll records until late in the evening in a very seductive manner. On other occasions he has beaten her. He recently blackened both of her eyes when she provoked him with threats of becoming a prostitute. She ran away from home after this beating. When she returned he brought her to Children's Court. She was subsequently referred to this institution.

Interview with Deborah.   Deborah is a rather precocious, buxom youngster who can easily pass for 18. Her physical build and her bleached hair convey an impression of promiscuity. However, she also has an infantile quality which elicited a sympathetic, protective attitude from this listener. She has been quite delinquent recently and readily admitted to having sexual relations with numerous boys and men and drinking intoxicating liquor. She also admitted that she has provoked some of the boys she dated to hit her and has often teased them sexually.

When asked about her family, she denied any guilt about her mother's death and any feelings, positive or negative, about her parents. She stated that although her younger siblings like her, she feels indifferent about them and prefers not to be bothered with them. She feels that there is something wrong with her father and blames him for most of her difficulties. She feels that he has no control over her because he vacillates between being overly strict and being too lenient with her and never expects anything from her consistently. She sees him as a hypocrite who is engaged in a battle of wills with her. She feels that although he says he does things for her sake he really puts his own interests first; moreover, he blames her for her mother's death when she died as a result of leukemia. In contrast to this, she said that she liked and trusted the male psychiatrist whom she had been seeing before she ran away. It is interesting that she does not care for liquor and drinks it only when she goes out with men or when her father offers her a drink.

Throughout the interview she spoke without any visible signs of emotion. Before she left she stated that if we removed her from her home and present school she would give up her education and go to work when she returns to the community.

Although she assumes a general façade of indifference and cynicism with adults, she had developed a positive relationship during her brief treatment contacts and seems to be seeking protection and guidance from adults.

Interview with the father. The father stated that he is afraid that Deborah might have an adverse effect on his other children, who present no problems. He complained that she is completely unmanageable. She has often stayed out until four or five in the morning without giving him an account of her whereabouts. She has refused to go away to summer camp with her two sisters because she wants to go to summer school to make up the math course she failed and has threatened to sleep with someone and get pregnant if he forces her to go. He has threatened to chain her to her bed as the only remaining way of controlling her. He will be relieved to have her out of the house because he is afraid that he might actually have to go through with his threat.

Report from the Detention Center

Although Deborah had asked her father not to visit her, he often did so. However, he refused to talk to any of the professional staff during his visits.

Education

Deborah had been in her second year at a high school for gifted students. She has superior intellectual ability, but this was not reflected in the grades she received during her first year of high school:

SUBJECT	GRADE	
	1st half	*2nd half*
English	80	80
Social Studies	85	85
General Science	90	85
Algebra	70	50
French	80	65
Laboratory Science	—	75
Art	80	80
Health	65	65

INFORMATION OBTAINED DURING HER EARLY MONTHS AT THE INSTITUTION

Initial Interview with the Principal

Deborah, a rather heavily built, bleached blonde, came into the office, stood by my desk and did not sit down until asked. I spoke to her about her previous school, which was a special school for gifted children. She told me she had been in the third term and had completed the following subjects during her first year:

SUBJECT	GRADE	
	1st half	*2nd half*
English	85	85
General Science	90	90
Algebra	85	30
Social Studies	90	90
French	85	75

She said that she had not been a good student in high school because the curriculum had been so unchallenging that she had not invested much time in it and hoped that this would not be the case here. She said that she liked school very much and had spent as much time there as possible. She felt that she was able to get something out of both the classroom work and the extracurricular activities at school. I asked her how she spent her time out of school. She said that she liked to listen to rock-and-roll and popular music, and also liked to go to dances. She stated that she enjoyed reading when she had the opportunity to do so. She liked to participate in sports, particularly volleyball and basketball. She enjoyed participation in student government, was a member of the student group in charge of the student lounge, and had been an opinion poller and a booster. I asked her about her vocational ambitions. She said that she had originally thought about law but probably would enter one of the scientific fields. She said that she did not want to study law because it would involve additional schoolwork after she had completed her bachelor's degree. She was not interested in art or music. She did have an interest in doing some simple craft work as she had done in public school and was interested in knowing whether she could continue her French course and whether it would be possible for her to learn mechanical drawing. It was quite obvious that she obtained a great deal of satisfaction from telling me that the school was for gifted children and that she was one of them.

I explained some of the school rules to her and asked her about her attitude toward boys. She immediately told me that sex was her problem, that she was here because she had had intercourse with a great many older men, some of whom were married. She said that since she had paid her penalty for her delinquent behavior while in the detention center, we had no right to keep her here. She also assured me that whatever took place here, once she returned to the normal school she would be exactly as she had been before she had come. She said that she was going to convince us that there was little we could do, if anything, to change her because she had no desire to be here in the first place.

Psychological Testing

Deborah was very pleasant and friendly throughout the testing. She stated that she wanted to be enrolled in the academic program because she wanted to graduate from high school.

She was given the intermediate form of the arithmetic achievement tests because of her own hesitation and anxiety about her arithmetic skills and the advanced form of the others. All these tests were extremely easy for her. She achieved a perfect score in arithmetic reasoning and made only one error in arithmetic computation. Her overall level of school achievement is approximately two years above her age level.

The projective tests reveal a picture of a self-centered youngster who has grandiose illusions of her own importance and who, at least superficially, is sophisticated. One of her major

areas of difficulty centers about her precocious sexual development and the anxiety she feels about it. She also appears to
have difficulty in understanding and controlling her aggressive
feelings. She may find herself feeling that she has little control
over her actions when she acts aggressively toward others.
There are also some suggestions that she may feel guilty about
things she has done in the past and use denial as a way of
dealing with her guilt.

There are indications that some of this youngster's social
poise and alertness may be more defensive than real. There
are also signs that under pressure she may evince illogical
kinds of thinking. Although not grossly pathological, this may
lead to impulsive behavior which she may be unable to control. She also appears to desire to be fed and cared for psychologically and to be unable to tolerate frustration, perhaps
because her needs in these areas were not met in the past.

All in all, she appears to be a very bright, self-centered, and
somewhat sophisticated youngster who has many basic anxieties and doubts about herself which may give rise to impulsive
behavior. She is obviously ready to complete the tenth-grade
academic program and appears to be well motivated for it.
However, her self-centeredness, her tendency to demand attention, and her inability to tolerate frustration may create problems in a group situation because she may not be aware of or
concerned with the needs of the other students.

Initial Psychiatric Interview

Deborah began by complaining that the school is boring,
that the institution is more like a prison than a rehabilitation
center, and that the staff members are more like wardens than
people who want to help others. Then she informed me that
she was "going to get out of here as soon as possible" and
would become pregnant because she had been incarcerated for
a crime she had not committed. Later she stated that if she
has to have a psychotherapist she would prefer a strong male
because she likes boys who do not let her pull the wool over
their eyes.

Psychotherapy Summaries: March to June

Initial interview. She entered in an extremely seductive manner. She told me in various ways not to waste my time trying to involve her in treatment. After a while, she attempted to engage me in a debate about whether a person has the right to behave destructively despite her father's wishes if she hurts only herself. I declined the challenge and stated that a father who allows a child to do so is breaking the law and has to be taken to court.

Two months later. She had been setting a trap for me. In a number of recent sessions she repeatedly told me about the delinquent behavior she had planned for her forthcoming home visit. Then she expressed her fears that I would inform the school authorities of her plans and she would lose her home visit. I commented that she had set a trap for me. If I informed the school authorities, I would be an untrustworthy "rat." If I did not, I would be allowing her to behave in a self-destructive manner. After I had encouraged her to examine her own motives, she decided to change her delinquent plans.

COMMENTS

1. What were Deborah's major underlying problems?

Most of Deborah's difficulties were related to her anxiety arising from self-doubts, her strong sexual and aggressive impulses, her desire for immediate gratification and her guilt about her own behavior.

2. What defenses and interpersonal techniques did she use to cope with her problems? How effective were they?

Anxieties arising from self-doubts. Her primary defense against her self-doubts was reaction formation. Through reaction formation, instead of feeling anxious, she had grandiose ideas about her importance and ability, was continually making others aware that she had attended a school for gifted children, maintained a façade of sophistication, and was sure that she did not have any problems. When reality broke through her reaction formation, she employed rationalization as her second line of defense. This was most evident when she attributed her less-than-exceptional achievement in school not to her own lack of effort and ability, but to the unchallenging curriculum. Occasionally when reality broke through her defenses, she coped with her anxieties and fears through avoidance. This was most evident in her hesitancy about the advanced form of the arithmetic achievement test.

Sexual feelings.   Deborah's sexual problems seem to have resulted from her own precocious sexual development plus her father's arousal of them through his relationship with her. If this were true, then her sexual misadventures can be thought of as defensive displacements of her sexual feelings for her father onto others. The fact that she was attracted to older men and has provoked her boyfriends to hit her as her father had done supports this hypothesis.

Although these displacements defended her against her sexual feelings for her father, they created additional problems. They aroused guilt against which she had to defend herself and caused difficulties between her and her father and between her and the law.

Aggressive impulses.   The psychological data suggest that Deborah was unable to defend herself against her aggressive impulses. She was unable to repress them and she was probably unable to inhibit their expression.

Desire for immediate gratification.   Deborah was unable to cope with her desires for immediate gratification. These desires created problems of major proportions for her because, unlike most people who learn to accept frustrations by the time they reach adolescence, she was unable to do so. Instead of accepting the fact that compromise and adjustment are necessary, she attempted to make others adjust to her. This was manifested in her difficulties at home, as well as in her provocative "you cannot make me" challenges to the staff of the institution. Sometimes she moved toward adults to gain her desires. At other times she attempted to intimidate them with threats of becoming pregnant or quitting school.

Guilt about her behavior.   Deborah did not feel guilty

about her behavior because she defended herself against such feelings through reaction formation. Instead of concealing her sexual misadventures and delinquent behavior, she flaunted them as if she were proud of them.

When her behavior is viewed as a totality, it is clear that although she was unable to defend herself against her sexual and aggressive impulses, her defenses were very efficient in protecting her from any anxiety, guilt, or shame about the way she acted them out. She actually regarded her behavior as expressions of desirable aspects of her personality, not as discomforting symptoms. Thus, although much of her behavior was maladaptive, we can understand why she felt that "once she returned to the normal school she would be exactly as she had been before she came here."

In this discussion we have focused exclusively on Deborah's emotional problems and her attempts to cope with them. Actually this has provided us with only an incomplete understanding of her behavior. We must also consider the self-actualizing aspects of her actions. For example, her active participation in extracurricular activities, her concern with being a gifted student, and her high academic goals can be thought of as reaction formations, but the contribution of the drive to actualize and fulfill her superior intellectual potential to such behavior should not be underestimated. The reason for focusing on her threatening feelings and the defenses and interpersonal techniques she used to cope with them is that they have particular relevance for the kinds of problems she had.

3. What kinds of educational difficulties might occur because of her problems?

Deborah's self-doubts could lead to academic difficulties despite her excellent taskability. She would be especially likely to avoid mathematics because of her insecurity about her ability in this area. She might avoid other areas of the curriculum as well if she felt threatened by them.

However, most of her difficulties in class would probably be interpersonal rather than academic. Her strong sexual impulses might make it difficult for her to adjust to a heterosexual class because the presence of boys could stimulate her to behave in ways that led her to her previous sexual misadventures. Her inability to tolerate frustration could easily bring her into conflict with her teachers because of her inability to accept compromise and delay. These necessary frustrations would also probably evoke many aggressive feelings in her which could result in hostile behavior because of her inability to inhibit her aggression.

4. What are the significant factors an educator should consider in attempting to deal with the problems discussed above?

There are three major factors an educator should consider in attempting to deal with the problems Deborah might present.

Since Deborah has succeeded in defending herself against many of her true feelings, there would probably be a discrepancy between her true motives and her perceptions of them. In fact, her defenses may have become such an integral part of her character that she might be unable even to entertain the possibility that she has misperceived her actions or those of others. In addition, she is also quite comfortable with her distortions and disinclined to change. Obviously the teacher who is confronted by the necessity of dealing with her web of reaction formations and rationalizations would be hard pressed to break through it. Any breakthrough would require consistent behavior on his part to discourage her distortions as well as the cooperation of her therapist in a joint effort to help her become cognizant of them.

Deborah has the potential for two different kinds of "acting out" behavior. She has the capacity for uncontrolled impulsive behavior as well as the potential for some consciously controlled "acting out" designed to induce others to satisfy her desires. The educator needs to distinguish between these superficially similar but dynamically different forms of behavior.

Transference relationships of three sorts are likely. Her "stubborn defiance" of her father, her flaunting of her delinquency, and her defiant challenge to the principal suggest the possibility of transference problems with her teachers centering around issues of control. Her grandiose notions of her importance and ability portend of transference around issues of receiving praise, attention, respect, aid, and so on. Her sexual misadventures with older men and her relationship with her psychiatrist suggest the possibility of a strong attachment to male teachers with sexual overtones. The transference possibilities are such that they could either facilitate or impede her education. Although the kind of transference which might develop would depend primarily upon Deborah, the educator's behavior could have a contributing influence. He should consider this in determining how he will handle the various problems she presents.

II

Deborah had already been at the institution for a few months during which time she completed her second year of high school. At the outset of her third year of high school her program was as follows: biology, world history, English and commercial subjects. During the first few months of her third year none of her classes were co-educational.

First Term: November

Commercial teacher (Mr. Kelly). Deborah makes constructive use of her time. She likes to work on the electric typewriter and gets to work as soon as she comes into the room. She has shown some ability and is making good progress in this subject. She has also learned to operate the various mimeograph and duplicating machines. However, although I have asked her on numerous occasions if she would like to learn to use the adding machine, she has made no effort to do so, stating that it is not related to her vocational goals. She responds well to me and has been extremely well behaved and cooperative in all respects. She has little to do with the other students and vice versa. She is so quiet and unobtrusive that often I have been unaware of her presence in class.

Social studies and English teacher (Mr. Williams).

Deborah has been doing exceptionally well in her studies. She has never caused any difficulty in class and takes pride in being a "mature, young adult."

Biology teacher (Mr. Roth).   Deborah received a very complimentary report from him as well. (Unfortunately it was subsequently misplaced.)

Second Term

At the start of the second term the biology, social studies, and English classes were made coeducational. The commercial class continued as before.

Social studies and English teacher (Mr. Williams): April. Debbie is an extremely bright student. Academic work poses no problems for her with the exception of current events discussions, in which she does not participate. She claims that she is not interested in discussing world problems, but the real reason for her disinterest is her lack of knowledge. She is very mark-conscious and sets very high academic goals for herself.

During the first term Deborah acted like any other normal teen-ager but almost immediately after the class became coed she started to act up. She would hum rock-and-roll songs out loud, snap her fingers in a "cool" manner, and act as if she were a member of a gang of juvenile delinquents instead of a member of a social studies and English class. However, even when she disrupted the class in this way, she was soon ready to get back to work, probably because she was so mark-conscious. Then she would say, "Okay, let's shut up now," or "Okay, you can continue now, Mr. Williams." Unfortunately, some of the other students, especially Joan, could not regain their composure as easily as she. I have told her that I do not need her help in running the class. I privately pointed out to her how she incited others to get into difficulty. However, although she willingly acknowledged that her behavior had been disruptive, she maintained that she could not hold herself responsible for the inability of others to control themselves. When our private conversations failed, I tried to discourage her disruptive behavior by punishing her. This was not effective. I then confronted her with her actions in front of the group. This merely made her more adamant and disruptive. She retaliated by convincing some of the other students that I had misjudged her and blamed her for my own inability to control the class.

When I attempted to keep her in the classroom during the coeducational recess because of her disruptive behavior, she told me that she would not remain in class because she would be very nervous if she missed her smoke break. When this did not sway me, she accused me of acting unfairly. She granted the justice of my keeping her from the recess but insisted that it would be unjust for her to miss her smoke break. Knowing that I could not allow her to smoke in class, she asked me to allow her to do so. When I refused she ran out of the room screaming curses at me. She went to the principal and then to her therapist and attempted to convince them that she had been treated unjustly. Later the principal, her therapist, and I discussed the incident and I decided not to punish her but to follow another tack instead.

When her psychotherapist became engaged in a project which prevented him from seeing Deborah during regularly scheduled hours, she and I became involved in another battle. She attempted to force me to allow her to leave the room in order to find out whether her psychotherapist could see her and would threaten to curse and scream if I did not. Whenever I refused, she did curse and scream and she blamed me for making her behave that way. Then she would stop and ask me if I really wanted her to continue this behavior. When I replied that I could not hold myself responsible for her disruptive conduct, she became enraged, lost control of herself, and cursed profusely. After a number of unsuccessful episodes of this sort, she gave up her attempt to intimidate me and I agreed to cooperate with her attempts to find out if her therapist could see her.

Now she is functioning well again. I believe that she should be allowed to attend school off grounds in the fall because she is a capable student and has a strong drive to do well. If she does, special care should be taken to place her in a class which will challenge her intellectually. Otherwise, she may become bored and difficult to manage.

Final report: June. Deborah is an extremely bright girl who should do well in college. Except for a few short periods Deborah was not a problem in class. In fact, she helped some of the other students review for their exams during afterschool hours. On a few occasions during the second term, especially when she wanted to see her psychotherapist and I would not excuse her, or when she was required to miss her recess period, she was very stubborn and unwilling to accept my decisions. At these times she would try everything possible to get her way. However, for the greater part of the term she functioned as well as any student could be expected to do. She should do very well in any of her future academic work.

Biology teacher (Mr. Roth): April. During the last few months Deborah's every thought has been concerned with seeing her psychotherapist. When she knows that he is at school, she is unable to concentrate on anything but seeing him. If she sees him, her classroom behavior is affected by how she feels about her session. If she does not see him, she becomes disorganized and upset. She will do anything and everything to see him. I have been surprised by some of the ingenious plots she has contrived recently.

Deborah lives for the immediate moment. She seldom tries to control herself and demands instantaneous gratification. When I refuse one of her requests—to find out if her therapist is on grounds, for example—she gets upset and tells me that she needs an answer because she is emotionally disturbed. Her usual comment when she has caused a disturbance is, "What do you expect from me? I am emotionally disturbed. That is why I am here."

Deborah has been waging a constant battle to demoralize me, disrupt the class, and frustrate my ambitions. She demands answers to obviously unimportant questions and when I confront her with her facetiousness, she denies it. Now when she does this I insist that she stop immediately or leave the room.

She refuses to obey me and even talks down to me. She has actually told me that she is too intelligent to learn anything from me. I have had to bring her down to size by telling her that the world does not revolve around her. She schemes, connives, and uses every device to exploit others. She is eager to receive but cannot give. She is quick to criticize but unable to accept criticism. She incites the other students into misbehaving and enjoys seeing them get into trouble.

She works only in areas in which she is sure to excel and adamantly refuses to try other things. She hands her work in late, often misses class, and makes almost no effort to improve or to control her emotions. Although she intends to go to college, I do not see how she will be able to do so if she continues to behave as she does. I find that being firm is the only successful way to deal with her. Therefore, I feel that she should not be given a passing grade, despite her ability to cram for tests, until her attitude and behavior improve.

Final report: June. Debbie's intellectual functioning was excellent. She was able to memorize pages and whole chapters in short periods of time. However, she has a number of difficulties which interfered with her overall functioning. She was obsessed with the desire for complete perfection. When disappointed academically, she became depressed, tense, and extremely disorderly. Her behavior was even more extreme when she was disappointed by her therapist. Recently, after she had been informed that her therapist had not come to work, she came into the room cursing at everyone and everything. She began to tear paper, break pencils, and shake her head and hands. Suddenly she began to scream and threw her desk to the floor. Finally it became necessary to have someone remove her from the room.

During the term she tried to impress the rest of the class by relating her delinquent experiences prior to coming here. In fact, she insisted that I treat her as an adult rather than like the other students. When I did not, she became very frustrated and disruptive. I approached her on the basis of the demands of the situation. When she was upset, I did not sympathize with her or reduce my demands. I told her how she was harming herself and insisted that she conform. This did not quiet her at the time, but her disruptive episodes lessened and became less dramatic over time. When she tried to manipulate me I did not allow her to succeed. A firm "No" accompanied by a statement such as "Stop trying to manipulate the situation!" was most effective. At these points she usually recognized that I was "on to her," laughed, and feigned a look of guilt in an attempt to get out of the situation.

She acted as if the only rules and regulations she accepted were those that suited her. I tried to face her with the fact that she would soon be leaving here and no school would tolerate her loss of control and disruptive emotional behavior. Since her mind was made up that she could behave one way here and another way somewhere else, my comments seemed to have little effect.

She attained a 95 on the state-wide exam and a 90 on the class final. Her final grade, based on her achievement and behavior, is 87.

Commercial teacher (Mr. Kelly): April. Deborah continues to function very well. As soon as she steps into the room she begins to work and consistently uses her time very well. She is quiet in class and has little to do with other students. She has shown a real interest in developing her typing ability and is already preparing for the state-wide examinations. Although she has not shown a great deal of aptitude in typing, she has made considerable progress because of her interest and consistent effort. She responds very well to me and has told me that she likes me. On occasion when a student becomes difficult, Deborah champions my cause. When she first came into the commercial class she refused to do her sweeping assignment; she now does not hesitate to do any of her job assignments. Although she has learned to operate the mimeograph and duplicating machines, she is not interested in anything except improving her typing ability and in passing the state-wide examination.

Final report: June. Deborah continued to function very well during this period. Her attitude, behavior, and work habits were excellent. She made very good progress in her typing. She made consistent effort in her preparation for the state-wide examination and should do well in it. In the classroom she was a model student. There was never any need to prompt her to work and she never presented a management problem. Her attitude toward me was excellent and she got along very well with the students. She has shown no real interest in anything other than her typing and has stated that this was only because typing was related to her vocational goals.

Grades

SUBJECT	STATE-WIDE EXAMINATIONS	FINAL GRADES
English	88	90
Biology	95	87
World History	92	93
Typing	95	90

COMMENTS

The material in Part I suggested that Deborah's major problems were related to anxieties arising from self-doubts, strong sexual and aggressive impulses, a desire for immediate gratification, and guilt about her actions.

1. How did these personality characteristics cause educational difficulties for her?

Self-doubts. Because of her self-doubts, Deborah was unable to venture where she anticipated failure. She avoided the adding machine, current events discussions, and certain aspects of the biology curriculum probably because she believed that she could not succeed in these areas.

Strong sexual impulses. Her strong sexual impulses, which were stimulated by the entrance of the boys into the class, also led to considerable difficulties. Prior to the arrival of the boys she was a model student. As soon as the class became coeducational she began to behave like a gang member. As she asserted her leadership in her fancied gang, she disrupted the classroom proceedings and challenged her teachers' position of authority. This brought her into conflict with them over the issue of who would control whom.

Aggressive impulses. Her inability to inhibit the expression of her aggressive feelings worsened her already strained relationships with her teachers. If she had been able to inhibit the aggression she felt toward her teachers because of their attempts to control her behavior, her classroom problems would have been less severe. Unfortunately, because she was not able to do so, they were exacerbated.

Desire for immediate gratification. Her desire for immediate gratification created classroom problems because it prevented her from adjusting to the uncertainties of her therapist's schedule. The anxiety which she felt about not knowing whether she would see him prevented her from concentrating in class and drove her to employ disruptive methods to find out whether he was able to see her. It also engendered anger against him which she unfortunately displaced onto her teachers.

Guilt about her behavior. In order to protect herself against feeling guilty about her disruptive behavior, she rationalized her actions by believing that she was the victim of unfair and callous teachers. When she so accused them, she strained her already tense relationships with her teachers even further.

2. How might the educator attempt to deal with the following?

Her unwillingness to work in certain areas of the curriculum.
Her reaction to the entrance of the boys into the class.
Her reaction to her psychotherapist's irregular schedule.

Her unwillingness to work in certain areas of the curriculum. Although the academic self-doubts which underlay Deborah's unwillingness to work in certain areas of the curriculum were inappropriate, it would be extremely difficult for the educator alone to extinguish them. Telling her that they were inappropriate would not help. His words would sound beside the point to her because she had concealed her self-doubts from herself through rationalizations. Nor would it help to attempt to demonstrate to her that they were inappropriate by forcing her to succeed in spite of them. For if the educator were to demand that she work in these areas despite her underlying anxiety, she would probably react negatively toward what she would perceive as unfair demands. Even if he coerced her into fulfilling his demands, she would probably be so immobilized and disorganized by her anxiety that she would fail just as she failed algebra. A solution to the problem would probably require the cooperative efforts of the therapist and the educator. The therapist would help her overcome her anxiety by making her cognizant of her rationalizations and anxieties and helping her to appreciate their inappropriateness. The educator would encourage her to examine her behavior in her therapy sessions by noting his disagreement with her rationalizations without, of course, attempting to convince her of their inappropriateness. As she became able to tolerate small doses of anxiety, the educator would use every means at his disposal to involve her in these areas in limited ways. The limited success she would gain in these areas in this way would corroborate the insights she had gained in therapy about the inappropriateness of her self-doubts. This might also enable her to tolerate greater degrees of involvement.

Her reaction to the entrance of boys into the class. Since Deborah did not conceal from herself the inappropriateness of her disruptive reaction to the presence of boys in the class and was able to control her behavior when she wanted to, the educator should deal differently with this problem. He should confront her with the inappropriateness of her actions, explain why they cannot be tolerated in class, and insist that she control them. Since these steps, if successful, would suppress only the behavior in question and not the emotion underlying it, another behavioral response to the emotion would probably take its place. Therefore, the educator must take additional steps to ensure that this response is a more desirable one. The leadership qualities she had demonstrated and her expressed wish to be treated as a mature student suggest that encouraging her to assume a more positive leadership role in the class could provide a desirable alternative. Commenting to her about the self-destructive effects of her present behavior might also encourage her to examine its origins in psychotherapy.

Her reaction to her psychotherapist's irregular schedule.
The emotions which underlay Deborah's reactions to her
therapist's irregular schedule were anxiety and anger. She was
anxious because of her uncertainty about whether she would
be able to see him and became angry whenever she discovered
that she would not. Her anxiety prevented her from concentrating on her schoolwork and drove her to contrive devious
plots to end it. Her anger also interfered with her concentration and created additional problems when it was displaced
onto her teachers.

The educator can relieve much of Deborah's anxiety by
establishing a procedure through which she can be apprised
of her therapist's arrival and availability. Assuaging part of
her anxiety in this manner should lessen the necessity for her
"plots" and also enable her to concentrate to a greater extent
on her work. Unfortunately the educator cannot do the same
thing with her anger about her therapist's unavailability because he cannot change his schedule. Since he cannot deal with
the origin of her anger, he must deal with her angry behavior.
Obviously Deborah could not concentrate on her schoolwork
when she was angry, but could she contain the anger which
she so readily displaced onto others? The psychological reports
suggest that she could not. If this is true, the educator must
decide whether to tolerate her outbursts in the classroom until
they have run their course or to remove her from the room
until she can contain herself.

Since she could not contain her feelings, whichever choice
he makes, he should not try to force her to suppress them nor
respond punitively to their expression. A punitive response
would confirm her distortions that he is worthy of her hostility
and probably prolong her outbursts by providing grist for
their mill. On the other hand, he might be able to discourage
her displacements by stating that he is aware that she is angry
and has difficulty controlling herself.

Hopefully the educator's efforts to facilitate rather than
obstruct her efforts to see her therapist and his acknowledg-
ment of her anger about not being able to do so would belie
her perception of him as "unfair and unfeeling." If it does

not, the principal should avoid being induced into commiserating with Deborah about her teacher's unfairness and the therapist should help her to become aware of the inaccuracy of her perceptions.

3. How appropriate were Mr. Roth's and Mr. Williams' attempts to deal with Deborah's difficulties?

Mr. Roth. Mr. Roth's general approach to Deborah's difficulties left much to be desired. He concentrated almost all his remedial efforts on persuading and coercing her to inhibit the expression of her feelings. He completely neglected any attempt either to assuage her underlying emotions or to provide her with more desirable forms of coping with them. His approach was inappropriate for a number of reasons.

Not realizing that she had excused much of her disruptive behavior through rationalizations, he made numerous futile and exasperating attempts to convince her that it was undesirable. Since he mistakenly believed that she was able but unwilling to control all of her disruptive behavior, he attempted to force her to do so, declined to facilitate her attempts to learn about her therapist's availability, and refused to modify any of his expectations despite the need to do so. Having attributed hostile motives to her actions, such as the wish to exploit others and demoralize and frustrate him, he vindictively "cut her down to size" in front of her peers, lowered her final grade because of her behavior, and failed to capitalize on her desire to be treated as an adult. As a result, he became enmeshed in a web of transference problems which endured throughout the term.

Mr. Williams. Mr. Williams' approach to Deborah's difficulties was similar to Mr. Roth's in many ways, probably because, like him, he initially believed that Deborah could have controlled much of her disruptive behavior and he was unaware that she believed her rationalizations. When persuasion failed, he too attempted to coerce her by confronting her in front of the class or punishing her.

This could have led to the development of the same kind of poor relationship between him and Deborah that existed between her and Mr. Roth. However, for a number of reasons, their relationship was never quite as bad and soon improved. First, unlike Mr. Roth, Mr. Williams did not attribute capricious and hostile motives to Deborah's actions. He did not believe that she exploited others, but that she was better able to regain her self-control. He did not perceive her rebellion against his authority as arbitrary but as a result of the entrance of the boys, or his confronting her in front of her peers. Second, unlike Mr. Roth, he was able to stop his coercive efforts when they proved fruitless. Third, unlike Mr. Roth, he finally agreed to facilitate her attempts to learn about her therapist's availability, though he had originally engaged in a power struggle with her.

4. What might account for the lack of any difficulty between Deborah and Mr. Kelly?

This might have been due to any one or more of the following:

Since the commercial class was not coeducational, the kinds of problems which arose in relation to delinquent behavior did not occur. The class was geared to a more individualized program of study which enabled the teacher to allow Deborah to work at her own pace. The commercial teacher did not force her to involve herself in tasks which she preferred to avoid. He thereby circumvented any conflict which might have ensued if he had.

5. Was Deborah ready to enroll in an American history course in an off-grounds summer school?

The risk involved in sending Deborah to summer school was not that she was ill equipped intellectually. It was that she might revert to her delinquent behavior out of class if she had not acquired enough inner control during her stay at the institution. Thus the decision was not one that the educator should make.

Deborah did attend the summer session. She completed one year of American history without incident and earned a 92 on the state-wide examination. Her cottage parents described her as a leader who influenced the other girls in a positive direction.

RECOMMENDED READINGS

Polsky's *Cottage Six* (1962) contains an incisive analysis of the effect of a delinquent peer culture on students' behavior. Cohen's *Delinquent Boys* (1955) presents a theory of delinquency based on social class differences. Sykes and Matza's "Techniques of Neutralization: A Theory of Delinquency" (1957) contains an alternative theory of delinquency as well as an analysis of the techniques which delinquents use to ward off guilt.

A penetrating psychoanalytic approach to the armor individuals erect against their feelings can be found in Reich's *Character Analysis* (1945). Fromm discusses various kinds of undesirable interpersonal relationships in his *The Art of Loving* (1956).

chapter 5

Ralph

I

BACKGROUND INFORMATION

Intake Summary: December, 1961.

Ralph is a fourteen-year-old boy who is being referred to us by a city hospital. He is a small, thin, anxious, and restless youngster with a history of emotional disturbances.

Interview with Ralph.   Ralph was quite eager to complain about his parents, whom he believes no longer care about his needs. The TV is broken, his father no longer takes him out, and he has to take money from his mother's purse because she does not give him a satisfactory allowance. He said that he gets so angry at them he feels as if he were about to explode and that they, not he, should be sent to an institution. When asked if he would be willing to go to the institution, he said he would be willing to go but was afraid that he would become homesick.

When asked about his peers he had little to say. He stated that he had a few friends, but preferred to stay home and work on his hobbies or watch TV.

Developmental history. Ralph was a breech baby. His mother remembers being afraid that she was choking him during the delivery. When weaning from the bottle was begun at seven months, he began to vomit solid foods. Throughout his childhood he would eat only certain foods prepared for him in specific ways and vomit everything else that was force-fed to him. Vomiting continued until he was well into the elementary grades. He often forced himself to vomit as a protest against parental demands and once, when he was three, refused to eat anything for ten days. He also vomited whenever his mother kissed or hugged him.

Terrified of insects, he was also afraid of having his nails trimmed or his hair cut, of going to the dentist, doctor, or school, and of riding on subways. He would often vomit on these occasions. As a result his mother would not feed him until he had returned from school or from other disturbing trips.

When he was nine he was brought to a child guidance clinic by his parents because of their inability to cope with him. At that time his mother stated that he derived a great deal of satisfaction from exhibiting himself to her, insisted that his parents meet his every demand, and behaved in an unmanageable fashion when they did not. He refused to allow his father to sleep during the day although the father worked nights, and threw lighted matches onto his parents' bed when he found them sleeping together. He refused to clean himself or change his underwear during the week, stating that it was foolish to put clean underwear on a dirty body. However, he ritualistically took a shower for one hour or more every Saturday evening. On these occasions he would demand a fresh piece of soap and would sit only on a special chair because he did not want to place his "clean body on any dirty furniture." When his father attempted to discipline him, Ralph would refuse to obey and would spit at him. Despite this, Ralph's mother was unwilling to accept the clinic's recommendation of placement in a residential treatment center.

His parents had him hospitalized when he was 13½ because his behavior had become increasingly intolerable. At this time his mother reported that when she did not acquiesce in his demands, he struck her, threatened her with knives and broken bottles, and said he would kill himself if she did not do as he wished. He often referred to her as "Jason" and would shout, "Jason, get me this! Jason, get me that!" The incident which led her to bring him to the hospital occurred when she refused to buy him a TV magazine. He broke his records, his phonograph, and some of the living room furniture, knocked her to the ground, and threatened to stab her with a knife he had picked up unless she agreed to buy the magazine for him.

While in the hospital he related well with his peers, was never a management problem, and adjusted satisfactorily to the hospital school. He admitted threatening his mother with a knife, but said it was just to scare her into giving him what he wanted and he would not have done anything with it.

Interview with the parents. Ralph's mother is a plump, careless, unkempt woman. During the interview she behaved in an aggressive, demanding manner and attempted to manage the discussion in accordance with her wishes. She seemed quite disorganized and at times her rambling speech became incoherent. She stated that she had brought Ralph to the hospital because she had been unable to cope with him. She volunteered that she had been quite punitive toward him in the past, beating him, smacking him across the face with a wet towel, and the like, and wondered if his behavior might be related to this. However, she did not think it unusual that until two years ago she allowed him to sleep with her at night after her husband had left for work and also examined his genitalia constantly to see if they were descending.

Ralph's father is a middle-aged man who is also the father of adult children from a previous marriage. He seems to be completely intimidated by Ralph and reacts to his behavior with fear, shortness of breath, and heart palpitations. He admitted that he has been sleeping in his car and on park benches during the day because Ralph will not allow him to sleep at home. He added that his wife also goes out during the afternoon in order to avoid Ralph. He appears to feel more warmly toward Ralph than his wife does, but he has been unable to assume a strong role in the family or to protect Ralph against his mother's physical abuse.

Ralph's parents have been unable to provide him with a healthy home. They are both disturbed and ineffectual. At home his behavior was grossly pathological; however, when he was away from home — at school, camp, or in the hospital — he was able to adjust satisfactorily. Residential treatment and continued removal from the home are strongly recommended.

Educational History

Ralph is in the ninth grade. His counselor reported that he gets along well with his teachers and peers and is liked by them. His academic performance is satisfactory and he is an active member of the school band. His seventh- and eighth-grade marks:

	7TH GRADE	8TH GRADE
English	80	80
Mathematics	65	70
Social Studies	80	80
Science	85	70
Physical Education	75	75
Music	90	90
Shop	65	65
Days absent	9	29

His achievement scores in eighth grade were Reading, 7.5; Arithmetic, 8.0.

Psychological Testing Prior to Admission

Ralph was exceedingly friendly, cooperative, and eager to please. He acted as if he expected something from me in return for his good behavior.

On the intellectual test he functioned within the average range with indications of bright-normal abilities. However, he manifested a number of difficulties. He approached in a trial and error manner the problems which required planning, foresight, and organization; he had difficulty with tasks involving judgment in and comprehension of social situations; and he reacted with blocking and confusion when his initial attempt was unsuccessful.

Ralph is a very anxious and insecure youngster who attempts to hide his anxiety behind a façade of intellectual capability and a screen of rationalizations. However, these maneuvers have succeeded only minimally and he is often all too cognizant of his difficulties. This was apparent in his need for reassurance each time he faced a difficult task and in his attempts to coerce the examiner into promising that she would not write down or show his "crazy, senseless answers to anyone." When threatened by the possibility of a failure experience which would reinforce his fear that he is worthless and inadequate, he resorts to withdrawal into pleasing fantasies. At these times it may be difficult to bring him back to the task at hand.

He seems more sensitive to his inner ideas and feelings than to his environment. As a result, he may behave in ways which have little to do with what is going on about him. Ralph is extremely fearful of authority figures whom he believes are poised to attack him. As a result he feels intensely hostile toward them and may, on occasion, act out his feelings. Classroom problems might also result from his anxiety and feelings of inadequacy, his inability to work under pressure for any length of time, and his tendency to be stimulated by group excitement. When he does act out for any of these reasons, he may be extremely difficult to reach through words and ideas. The only alternative may be to remove him temporarily to another environment. In general, Ralph appears to be a youngster with good intellectual abilities and educational skills. Academically, he is ready for a ninth-grade program. Emotionally, however, he is still extremely infantile and uncontrolled.

EVALUATION AT END OF SCHOOL YEAR

Ralph was admitted to the institution during November. At the end of the school year, he insisted that he was ready to attend the neighborhood high school. Since some staff members believed that he might be ready to do so, a complete evaluation of his readiness was made, including a report by his psychotherapist, psychiatric interview, psychological tests, and an interdisciplinary progress meeting.

Psychotherapist's Report

Ralph spent most of his initial sessions complaining about the staff, especially his cottage parents. He felt that they were spying on him, that the food was bad, and that there were not enough towels. After some months his comments changed. He reported that his cottage parents were doing nice things for him, such as taking him to town and buying him ice cream. However, he was sure that there was an ulterior motive behind their actions and he complained that his cottage father would not give in to him and that his cottage mother coaxed him to eat his food as his mother had done.

At the outset he maintained that the reason he did not make friends with his cottage mates was that he feared he would lose control of himself and hurt them when they criticized him, and bragged that he could beat up all of them except one. In later sessions he said he was sure that the reason he had few friends was they did not like him because he was inferior. He remarked that he had "only had one friend who was a creep" like himself because he could not play ball and did crazy things too. He blamed his parents for his difficulty in making friends because they had never taught him how to get along with kids. Then he added that he did not want friends anyway.

He thinks of himself as an inferior and crazy person. Although he often complains about the way his parents have treated him, his complaints do not assuage the strong guilt he feels about the way he was mistreated and manipulated them.

He was greatly relieved when he finally came to appreciate the fact that they, too, were responsible for the way he had acted.

Ralph is still a very anxious and suspicious youngster who believes that attack is imminent. He has made considerable progress in controlling his aggressive feelings, but the potential for outbursts of aggression is still present. His suspicion of the staff is probably a transference of a reasonable and perhaps necessary attitude toward his parents. Although this suspicious attitude still permeates his relationships, he is now able to see how it is based on and rationalized by distorted perceptions and illogical ideas.

He has become quite conforming in the cottage and is now quite passive and dependent in his relationship with his cottage parents.

Psychiatric Interview

Ralph spent most of the time telling me how much he had improved as a result of his short stay here. He said that he can watch the kind of adult TV programs his parents wanted him to watch and he can follow his cottage parents' requests even when they ask him to do the things he refused to do for his own parents. When asked why he had refused when his parents had asked him, he stated that he wanted to get even with them for the poor treatment they had given him. The reason for this attempt to convince me that he was healthier than before became clear when he asked me if I would send him home. When I told him no, he immediately asked angrily if the judge could send him home even if the institution thought he should remain.

Psychological Testing

Psychological tests were administered to help gauge Ralph's readiness to go off grounds to school.

In general, the present diagnostic picture confirms the prior diagnosis of an extremely disturbed youngster. However, some improvement is evident. There is somewhat less disorganization, blocking, and confusion, and the potential for unpredictable, violent, emotional outbursts has diminished slightly.

Ralph is presently an infantile and self-centered youngster. He has exaggerated illusions of his own ability which he uses to defend himself against severe feelings of inadequacy. His suspicious attitude, which serves him as an armor against an imagined hostile world, is on the increase. He is actively attempting to control his grandiose and suspicious ideas and make them conform to the reality about him. However, his ability to do this is still quite limited. As a result he reacts initially to people by withdrawing in suspicious fright. He can recover somewhat, but even then he continues to see them as ready to take advantage of him. Women are seen more positively than men and also as the persons to be turned to when he looks for external control. Men are seen as weaker and more "crazy." These perceptions seem to stem directly from his perception of his parents and he would probably tend to view our staff members in terms of them. Although he sees his therapist regularly and goes through the motions, he is probably not involved in treatment because his suspiciousness and grandiosity prevent him from engaging in meaningful relationships. There are times that he sees his therapist as someone to be manipulated and utilized for his own ends rather than as someone who can help him examine his ideas and feelings. It would be necessary for him to become involved in treatment before he would be ready to go off grounds to school.

He has been depressed for a long time because of his mistreatment at home and has become increasingly aware of his feelings. This has led to repetitive, morbid ideas of suicide and death. Care should be taken not to exacerbate his depression to the breaking point.

Ralph has superior intellectual potential, but because his own point of view interferes with his perception, and his feelings interfere with his functioning, he can achieve only at the normal level at best. If forced to perform, his functioning would probably deteriorate further, especially in terms of concentration, attention, and commonsense reasoning. His arithmetic and reading achievement scores indicate that his achievement is approximately one year below his grade level.

However, study skills testing indicated that he is far from ready to use his academic abilities.

Ralph does not appear to be emotionally, intellectually, or academically ready to attend an off-grounds school. His insistence on it reflects his grandiose and disturbed thinking. He will probably have difficulty mastering the curriculum of our own tenth-grade academic program.

Summary of Progress Meeting

Cottage parents. He was extremely uncooperative initially, but has been more cooperative recently. He teases and provokes his cottage mates and has few friends. He still demands too much attention and too many personal favors.

School report. Ralph completed our low-pressure ninth-grade academic course. He was very demanding and provocative and teased his peers excessively. He has become more cooperative during the past three weeks, but he still teases and maligns his peers and instigates trouble. He rarely participated in discussions and was quite isolated when not provoking his peers. He is a year behind in mathematics and reading, but passed all his courses. He probably could complete our tenth-grade program, but he is not ready for an off-grounds school.

Music teacher. He made excellent progress, but he fell apart after he had been told that he was doing well. He responded well to pressure and became overly dependent on his teacher to the point that he became a nuisance. He could profit from attending a music school this summer.

Decision. He should be allowed to attend an off-grounds music school this summer. However, he should remain on grounds during the forthcoming year.

COMMENTS

1. What were Ralph's major underlying emotional problems?

Ralph believed that he was a worthless and inadequate youngster whose world had been, and would continue to be, full of rejection, abuse, and imminent harm. Because of this belief he was extremely fearful of people, insects, subways, and so on; angry toward those whom he feared and anxious and depressed about his inadequacy and worthlessness.

2. What defense mechanisms and interpersonal techniques did he use to cope with each of these emotional problems? How effective were they?

Fear that others would reject, abuse, or attack him. At home Ralph moved against those from whom he feared harm. He provoked, attacked, dominated, and intimidated his parents. At the institution he continued to move against his peers and cottage parents, whom he suspected were about to harm him. Occasionally, for example during his interview with the psychiatrist, he moved toward others as a way of disarming them. However, when this did not succeed, he immediately reverted to moving against them, probably because this was his primary interpersonal technique.

Anger. Ralph did not control his anger. He neither repressed nor suppressed it, but gave vent to it readily. This was because his primary mode of interpersonal relationships was moving against others.

Anxiety and depression related to self-perceptions of inadequacy and worthlessness. Ralph's major defense against his feelings of inadequacy and worthlessness and their emotional concomitants was reaction formation. He erected an intellectual façade and set grandiose goals for himself which belied his self-perceptions. However, his academic skills were limited, and his intellectual façade did not supply him with the skills to achieve at a normal level, much less at the grandiose level he had set for himself. As a result, reality often threatened to break through his defenses. When this occurred he became extremely anxious and withdrew into a world of pleasant fantasies.

These techniques not only failed to defend him against the fear, anger, and anxiety which constantly beset him, but also created additional problems for him. His grandiosity and withdrawal into fantasy kept him out of contact with reality for considerable periods of time. His hostility toward others probably engendered hostility toward him. His ability to intimidate and dominate his parents made it unnecessary for him to grow up and left him with a reservoir of guilt about the way in which he had intimidated them.

In general, Ralph was an extremely suspicious, hostile, impulsive, infantile youngster whose behavior was determined more by the promptings of his inner emotions than by the requirements of his environment.

3. What educational difficulties might occur because of the problems described above?

On the basis of these problems, Ralph might be expected to have numerous educational difficulties.

His poor taskability — especially his thought disorders — should give rise to serious academic difficulties.

His tendency to move against others, his peers as well as adults, might lead to manifold discipline problems. This would be especially likely, considering the disruptive manner he used to intimidate others to acquiesce in his wishes.

The fear which pervaded his life may be expected to manifest itself in his classroom functioning and prevent him from dealing with many aspects of the curriculum. His tendency to withdraw into a world of fantasy whenever he felt threatened would make it even more likely that he would be unable to involve himself in many aspects of the curriculum.

The grandiosity and the intellectual façade he affected would probably lead him to strive for inappropriate goals and prevent him from acknowledging and thereby overcoming his educational difficulties. His inclination to try to earn special privileges by good behavior rather than by appropriate effort would reinforce his tendency not to deal with his difficulties.

In general, one can anticipate a multitude of difficulties resulting from the feelings of fear, anger, anxiety, and depression with which he was unable to cope.

4. What are the significant factors an educator should consider in attempting to deal with these problems if they arise?

Although it would be desirable educationally to help Ralph relate less to his grandiose goals and fantasies and more to his actual taskability, to do so could be quite dangerous. His defenses are already quite meager. If he were stripped of them, he might easily be overwhelmed by feelings of inadequacy and worthlessness. The anxiety and depression which might result from this could lead to self-destructive behavior, possibly even suicide. Therefore, it would be important for the educator to use extreme caution in any attempt to confront Ralph with the reality against which he has been defending himself.

Although Ralph was subject to **uncontrolled** outbursts of aggression and possibly even uncontrolled self-destructive behavior, he was also capable of threatening such behavior or actually resorting to it in a **purposeful** and **controlled** manner in order to induce others to acquiesce in his wishes. Therefore, when and if Ralph behaves aggressively, or threatens to do so, the educator must determine whether Ralph is able to control himself before he decides how to handle his behavior.

Although Ralph's perceptions of others were often distorted, he was sometimes able to correct them. The educator should determine whether Ralph is aware of his distortions before he attempts to deal with them.

II

Social Studies and English Teacher (Mr. Williams)

September: From a note written to the principal.   Ralph is extremely provocative. He takes things off my desk, calls me by offensive nicknames, and pretends that he can tell me what to do because he has been at the institution longer than I. He must realize that I will not permit this in class. May I see you about this?

November.   Ralph began acting antagonistic toward me after the second week of the term. He instigated others to behave disruptively, called me names, demanded that I follow his instructions and do things for him, and made hooting noises whenever I turned my back to the class. He attempted to bother me and, unfortunately, he succeeded. Whenever another student was upset and behaved inappropriately, Ralph could not prevent himself from joining in and adding to the commotion.

Recently, his behavior took a turn for the better as a result of my consistent refusal to accept his disruptive actions. He told me that, before the outset of the school year, he had decided to make trouble for his new teacher because he had not been permitted to attend a regular high school. He said he had felt that since he had been a good student last year without getting anything out of it, he was going to have fun in class this year. Now he is very industrious and cooperative. However, he demands too much immediate attention and acts as if he thought he were my boss.

Despite his statements and beliefs to the contrary, Ralph has considerable difficulty with his academic subjects. His spelling and reading are poor. He needs individual tutoring in these areas. He also has difficulty understanding relationships between events. He does not function well enough to attend a public high school, although he believes that he does.

Report card comments. Ralph's attitude has improved considerably during the past three weeks. I hope that he will keep it up. Grades: English, 70; World History, 65.

January. Ralph's behavior has changed markedly since my last report. As I began to confront him with his academic difficulties and he became aware of his failings, his attitude changed. He became terrified of every examination and every question. He insisted that his work should be kept from his fellow students and wanted me to promise not to show his work to anyone, especially his therapist. He blamed me for his failures and told me that I was a poor teacher and a crazy person. He stopped this after a few weeks when he realized that he could no longer get me angry this way. Then he began to threaten to drop the course. But when I repeatedly told him that I was not disturbed and did not feel threatened by the possibility of his leaving, these threats also ceased.

Now that he realizes what his difficulties are, he is very depressed and he has lost all interest in the subject matter. It does not appear that he will be able to complete the course.

Teacher's comments on his report card. Ralph's classroom

behavior has been improving. However, he does not take his behavior seriously enough. He has been working very hard, especially in English. Grades: English, 74; world history, 69.

April. Ralph and I have gotten along very well in recent months: this was not true in the past. At first, Ralph believed he knew everything. He is now afraid that he will fail and nothing I say can quiet his fear of this. He should not be encouraged to continue in the academic program next year.

He is very interested in music and often leads an imaginary band in class when he becomes anxious. Perhaps he might attend a music school next year and enroll in only a minimum of academic classes.

June. Ralph has worked very hard this year and he has made considerable progress. He completed all his assignments on time and wrote a number of extra credit reports without being asked to do so. However, he still has a great many educational problems. His study habits are atrocious. He skim-reads and uses the index to find answers instead of reading through the chapters of his history textbook. Most of his work, including his thirty-page extra credit report about ancient Egypt, was copied or paraphrased from textbooks. He was more interested in writing something down on paper in order to fulfill the requirements than in learning the work. Often his answers bore no relation to the questions posed. He was unable to generalize from one event to another and to conceive of events in terms of cause and effect relationships or in chronological order. He could not think things through, but jumped to immediate conclusions on the basis of insufficient evidence.

I tried to convince him to work on these problems, but to no avail. He preferred to expend his energy writing extra credit reports although I tried to discourage him from doing so. He seemed to have believed that if he inundated me with enough evidence of his efforts he would receive a passing grade. He kept asking me for reassurance that he would pass, but I could never give him enough of it.

Ralph will receive a 65 in both World History and English because of his effort, cooperation, and active participation in classroom activities. He should be continued in the eleventh-grade academic program in accordance with his wishes. However, since he has not overcome his academic problems, he will probably not do any better next year.

Comment on his final report card. Ralph worked very hard to pass World History and English. His efforts should be a standard for others. It would be helpful to him to improve his study skills. Grades: world history, 65; English, 65.

Biology Teacher (Mr. Roth)

January. Ralph is not interested in the biology curriculum. However, he has an intense curiosity about diseases. At the beginning of the term he constantly asked me questions about physical and mental symptoms which he imagined he had. I told him that I was a biology teacher, not a medical doctor. I suggested that if he really experienced the symptoms he reported, he should inform the infirmary staff. Ralph likes the role of class smart aleck and clown because of all the attention he receives. Sometimes he loses control of himself and I have to remove him forcibly from the class until he calms down.

Early in the term he expected to be an "A" student. Whenever he received a mark below 80, he would become upset and disruptive. Now that he expects to fail he becomes upset before every examination.

Ralph has very few friends in class because he is too ready to interpret his peers' actions as insults and affronts. This leads to many quarrels between him and others.

Report card comment. Ralph should make a greater effort to get along with his classmates. Grade: 75.

June. Ralph has not used his academic potential, although he has been careful to fulfill the minimum course requirements in terms of assignments and class participation. He has not shown much interest in his work. During the first few weeks of the course he used to ask the medical staff for help with his assignments so that he would not have to do them himself, but I soon put a stop to that. He even tried to force me to do his work for him.

His main difficulty was that his emotional problems interfered with his functioning. When any kind of physical disease was mentioned, he became extremely restless and uneasy, withdrew into a state of semiconsciousness and acted as if he were playing the piccolo or leading a band. On occasion, he became so involved in his fantasies that the only way I could gain his attention was by shaking him. On other occasions when he was anxious, he became so disruptive that I had to remove him from the room until we had begun a new topic. He pestered me for explanations of psychological terms which he thought might apply to him and seemed quite anxious if I told him what they meant. He was very provocative with his peers and with me. On several occasions he attacked other students, kicking and biting them and scratching their faces.

During the second term he attempted to get me to allow him to drop the course and threatened, if I did not, that he would behave so terribly that I would have to "get rid" of him. He supported his requests with statements to the effect that he did not need academic work to be a musician, that the work was too difficult, that he was too stupid to learn biology, that he wanted to be a printer and should have been in the print shop all day. Since Ralph was very insecure, my principal way of dealing with him was to reassure him that he could do the work and to tell him that he was not stupid. Of course, I also had to remove him from the class when he became so anxious that he could not control himself and had to be restrained physically.

It is clear to me that the only thing that kept Ralph going this year was the counseling that he received from his therapist, the school counselor, and others. For him to have attended an off-grounds school this year would have been a catastrophe. His periods of self-control and composure were too few and too short. He needed and still needs reassurance and complete acceptance because of his extreme lack of self-confidence. Perhaps then he might be able to use his potential.

Report card comment.   Ralph still needs to improve his conduct. Grades: State-wide examination, 59; course grade, 65.

Excerpt from Therapist's Report

October.   Ralph complained about his English teacher, whom he felt was crazy because his anger was so unpredictable.

He described how he was thrown into a state of panic every time his teacher was angry. He stated that it reminded him of how he himself used to get when he felt surges of uncontrolled anger and said that he anticipated the same kind of wild, uncontrolled behavior from his teacher. After exploring the matter he was able to see that this was a misconception on his part.

February.   He related an incident in the biology class in which he picked up a piece of laboratory equipment and threatened to stab one of the boys who he was sure was about to attack him. His version of the incident was quite different from that of his teacher. It was only after considerable exploration and discussion that he was able to see how he might have instigated the other youngster, who he felt hated him.

March.   Ralph arrived in a state of panic about his imminent failure in the academic program. He said that he felt completely worthless and incapable. He confessed that he had been copying and cheating since November and could no longer concentrate in class or understand anything that was going on. We discussed his desire to withdraw from the academic program and enroll in the vocational program. After a few sessions, he was able to see that if he completed the semester before changing programs he would have less difficulty obtaining a high school diploma.

COMMENTS

In Part I it was suggested that Ralph might have problems in school because of the following personality characteristics: poor taskability, feelings of worthlessness and inadequacy, pervasive fears, a tendency to use others primarily as objects for the satisfaction of his own needs, anger, guilt feelings about his behavior, and a potential for self-destructive behavior during periods of extreme depression.

In what ways did these personality characteristics contribute to his classroom difficulties?

Poor taskability.   The academic demands of the curriculum created problems of major proportions for Ralph because of his poor taskability. The list of problems compiled by his social studies teacher testifies to this.

Feelings of worthlessness and inadequacy. His underlying feelings of inadequacy and worthlessness prevented him from dealing effectively with his academic problems because they were too threatening to him. The academic year can be divided into two periods in terms of the ways in which he coped with the academic demands which threatened to arouse his feelings of inadequacy and worthlessness.

During the first period, when he was confronted by challenges which were beyond his capabilities, he defended himself against the anxiety which might have occurred through reaction formation. He refused to acknowledge that they were difficult for him, presented grandiose goals, and maintained his intellectual façade. In order to meet the challenges and hide his poor taskability, he tried to induce others to do his work for him, copied from textbooks, and so on. Although he did succeed in defending himself in this way against the anxiety which might have beset him, he did so at the expense of impeding rather than facilitating his educational progress.

The second period resulted from the constant demands of Ralph's teachers that he acknowledge his true taskability. These demands and confrontations belied his reaction formations. As a result his feelings of inadequacy and worthlessness broke through into awareness and he was inundated by anxiety. Stripped of his reaction formations, he attempted to rationalize his difficulties by blaming his teacher for them. However, this too did not succeed and his anxiety persisted. He then attempted to enlist his teachers' support in his struggle against his anxiety. He sought reassurance from them that he would not fail and tried to win their support through writing extra credit reports and conscientiously fulfilling all the requirements. But his teachers could not offer him enough reassurance to assuage his anxiety because that was produced by his feelings of inadequacy and worthlessness, not by his fear of failing. As a result, he remained anxious and depressed and tried to escape from the situation. He began to spend more of his class time in a world of fantasy and tried to force his teachers to "get rid" of him.

Fortunately, his teachers and his psychotherapist were able to help him with his panic and depression so that toward the end of the year his disruptive behavior, his attempts to be "gotten rid of," and his blaming of others for his difficulties diminished. However, although his behavior changed, he remained an anxious and self-doubting youngster for the remainder of the school year.

Pervasive fears.   Ralph's chronic fearfulness expressed itself quite often in the biology class when diseases were discussed. On these occasions he became quite upset and withdrew into his fantasies or acted disruptively, perhaps to invite his teacher to remove him from the class and the threatening topics being discussed.

Tendency to use others as objects for the satisfaction of his own needs.   Ralph often used others as tools to further his own purposes. He induced other staff members to do his work for him, instigated other students to do his disrupting for him, and attempted to force his teachers to "get rid of" him. If his teachers had allowed him to do all these things, he would have avoided coming to grips with his academic difficulties, and he would have escaped the responsibility for his own actions. Fortunately, his teachers, who were aware of what he was trying to do, refused to complement his actions.

Anger.   Ralph's undefended reservoir of anger needed little environmental stimulation to tap it. In fact, it seems that the transference of his anger toward his parents to others may have occurred without any basis in reality. He apparently was unable to suppress his feelings or inhibit their expression by himself but needed the additional external controls with which his teachers provided him. These outbursts of anger created numerous difficulties. They inflicted physical harm on other students, disrupted the class, and interfered with his educational progress. Happily, his teachers were able to supply him with the external controls he needed and as a result of their efforts and those of his therapist, most of these difficulties were minimal.

Guilt feelings about his behavior.   The available information suggests that guilt was not one of Ralph's major problems in school. However, he attempted to rationalize his disruptive behavior in various ways; he had been at the institution longer than his teacher, he had misbehaved because he had not been rewarded for his good conduct during the previous year, and so on, all suggesting that he did feel guilty about his actions. Perhaps the reason it was not a major problem for him was that he was able to defend himself through these kinds of rationalization.

The possibility of self-destructive acts. There were no incidents of self-destructive acts during the academic year. This was probably due, in large measure, to his teachers' and his therapist's efforts to reduce his anxiety and depression.

2. How might the educator attempt to deal with each of the following problems?

Grandiose self-concept and intellectual façade
Poor study techniques and taskability
Outbursts of aggression
Pervasive fears
Withdrawal into a world of fantasy
Threats to withdraw from the course

Grandiose self-concept and intellectual façade. Although it is educationally desirable to help Ralph achieve a more realistic appraisal of his educational taskability, the process of correcting his rationalizations and reaction formations may be a dangerous one. If Ralph is confronted with his feelings of worthlessness and inadequacy before he has acquired the means of coping with them, he could become extremely depressed and self-destructive.

The educator is not likely to be able to determine the rate at which Ralph would be able to face his feelings without any serious repercussions. Therefore, in order to avoid proceeding too rapidly, it would be imperative for him to work closely with Ralph's therapist. For the therapist usually has a more direct line to a student's emotional state and can best judge how necessary a student's defenses are to him.

The educator can help Ralph to need his defenses less by providing him with self-enhancing classroom experiences. He can provide him with success and acceptance at his own level, opportunities for concentration in areas in which he can achieve at a higher level, and occasions for integrating his exceptional musical talents into the classroom curriculum.

Poor study techniques and taskability. Ralph resorted to copying, to paraphrasing, and to inducing others to do his work for him because his difficulties in conceptualizing, abstracting, generalizing, and delaying judgments prevented him from completing his assignments in any other way. Therefore, the first thing an educator must do is reduce the intellectual demands placed on Ralph. This would enable him to succeed at his own level without having to resort to undesirable study techniques. Following this the educator can then help him to overcome his intellectual difficulties so that he can begin to function at grade level. Since habits are difficult for anyone to break and even more so for a youngster with as little self-control as Ralph, the educator would have to supplement Ralph's intentions to study properly by seeing to it that he does.

Outbursts of aggression. Since Ralph's aggressive outbursts resulted more from internal pressures and transferences than from external stimulation and reality, the educator's ability to discourage them through his own actions is quite limited. A successful assault on Ralph's transference would require the active cooperation of his psychotherapist. However, there are a number of steps which the educator could take in order to lessen this problem. He could discourage the development of transference to some degree by behaving in as nonthreatening manner as possible. He could discourage the outward expression of the transference by maintaining a vigilance for signs of developing hostility, by intervening early, and by employing the seating arrangements, physical plant, and the like, to best advantage. If Ralph acts aggressively despite this series of precautions, the teacher could still help him by intervening immediately. This could assuage Ralph's anxiety about losing control over himself. Punishing him for his behavior is, of course, an ever-present possibility. It could provide the additional external control which Ralph needed to suppress his anger. However, it could also impede his progress toward **self**-control and encourage the development of the kind of negative transference which could interfere markedly with his educational progress.

Pervasive fears. Since Ralph was unable to control the expression of his fears, the teacher should not exert pressure on him to do so. Not only would this be futile; it might also lead to further withdrawal and even more disruptive behavior. Instead, the teacher should help Ralph deal with his fears in more acceptable ways. He could encourage him to discuss the problem with his therapist, and he could provide him with alternative projects in the class or even in other classes when a threatening topic is broached. He could even provide him with advance notice of the topics to be covered to facilitate this. In these ways, he would enable Ralph to cope with his fears without withdrawing into fantasy or forcing the teacher to "get rid of" him. Of course, the teacher should explain to Ralph that although these modifications may be necessary at the time, they should not be abused, and he should be vigilant to see that they are not. He should also be prepared to help Ralph along the road toward facing his fears and dealing with threatening topics when and to the extent that he becomes able to do so.

Withdrawal into a world of fantasy. The steps taken to help Ralph deal with his anxieties and fears should reduce his need to withdraw. However, because they may not eliminate it, additional measures would be required: examples include attempting to keep his attention and interest focused on the matter at hand and making sure that it offers him a good chance for success. If, despite this, Ralph still withdraws, the teacher should call him back to attention as unobtrusively as possible, being careful not to create an amusing situation for the other students and an embarrassing one for Ralph. Above all, since this behavior is beyond his control, he should not be pressured to inhibit it or punished for not doing so.

Threats to withdraw from his classes. When Ralph threatened to withdraw from some of his classes unless his teachers acquiesced in his wishes, he faced them with a difficult problem. In dealing with it a teacher should first decide why Ralph made the threat. He might have been attempting to intimidate a teacher by threatening to behave self-destructively just as he intimidated his parents by threatening to commit suicide. He also might have been seeking to rationalize his desired departure from the class so as to avoid the realization that he was unable to cope with the curriculum.

If the teacher decides that the first is the more likely of the two explanations, he should treat the threats as he would any other manipulative attempt. However, if he believes that the second explanation is more likely, as it probably was, then another approach would be in order. This approach would call for a joint attempt by the teacher and the therapist to help Ralph examine the appropriateness of his demands on the teacher, the real basis for his desire to withdraw from the class, and the inappropriateness of his rationalizations.

3. How appropriate were his teachers' attempts to handle these problems?

In the main, his academic teachers did an excellent job. They realized that he was **unable** to do many things and did not attempt to force him to do the impossible. They did not confirm either his grandiosity or his perceptions of worthlessness and inadequacy. However they did force Ralph to face his true taskability faster than he was able. They provided him with both the reassurance and the external control he needed. They did not become involved in power struggles over his withdrawals, aggressions, or manipulations. They did not yield to his attempts to induce them to do his work for him and to assume responsibility for his actions.

In terms of constructive criticism, the social studies teacher might consider why he recommended that Ralph should be continued in the academic program despite his academic difficulties and the biology teacher might question whether he could have been more cognizant of these difficulties.

4. Should Ralph have been continued in the academic program during the eleventh year or transferred to a less demanding program?

The social studies teacher listed numerous academic problems which indicated that Ralph would do no better in the program that he had already done. The biology teacher underscored Ralph's insecurity in the program. This suggests that Ralph should have been transferred to a program in which he would be more successful and less anxious. Moreover, although Ralph now wanted to continue in the program, earlier in the term he himself had recognized his difficulties and had asked to be transferred. Continuing him in the program would merely confirm his grandiosity.

Ralph continued in the academic program during his eleventh year. However, after two months he asked for a change in program. A progress meeting was held with the following results.

Cottage parents' report.   Ralph was transferred to this cottage one year ago. He has been cooperative and self-reliant, but he demands unreasonable favors. He has no friends in the cottage and is disliked by almost everyone.

School report.   Ralph does not have the educational skills to complete an academic program. He does well in the print shop and is looking forward to a career as a printer if he can not succeed as a musician.

Therapist's report.   He became extremely depressed recently as a result of difficulties in the cottage and school and made a suicide attempt. If relieved of the academic pressures which gave rise to the depression, he would probably not attempt suicide again in the foreseeable future.

His relationship with his parents has not improved. His mother continues to keep him dependent on her and uses money as a weapon. He rightly feels that he has to fight and manipulate in order to obtain anything from them. He should not return home when he is discharged.

Recommendations

1. Transfer from an academic to a vocational program with emphasis on printing
2. Continuance of music lessons
3. Reevaluation in spring for possible discharge after the summer

chapter 6

Conclusions

In the preceding three chapters we discussed the education of three emotionally disturbed students in terms of their own unique personalities. In this chapter we will draw some general conclusions about the education of emotionally disturbed students from these individual case studies.

EDUCATIONALLY SIGNIFICANT
DIMENSIONS OF PERSONALITY

An awareness of the dimensions of personality along which emotionally disturbed students differ from normal students is basic knowledge for the educator. It helps to provide him with a systematic method for identifying emotionally disturbed students, uncovering their underlying problems, understanding their educational difficulties, and selecting educational solutions for them. Since the problems of disturbed students reflect their less than adequate capacity for meeting life's challenges and capitalizing on its opportunities for satisfaction, one way of discerning these dimensions of personality is to compare systematically the emotionally disturbed students' capacities in these areas with those expected of normal young-sters at the same stage of growth and development.

THE NORMAL STUDENT

The normal student is born with very limited capacities for meeting life's challenges and exploiting its opportunities. How-ever, his capacity for doing so is increased in a number of ways as he matures.

Reality Orientation

The maturing student is attuned to an expanded environ-ment. The unknown and the difficult arouse his curiosity; he actively involves himself in new endeavors which dare him to master them, and he is more responsive to the possibilities his environment offers for new forms of mature satisfactions. As a result, he is willing to sacrifice old forms of satisfaction for new ones. He is capable of entering into more mature rela-tionships with greater numbers of people. He actively seeks relationships with others for emotional rather than material gratification. He is capable of maintaining stable relationships with them, and is sensitive to their feelings and desires.

Reality Testing

The maturing student employs the knowledge he obtains from his expanded relationships with his environment in the service of his desires. His knowledge enables him to judge whether his desires are attainable; to determine which other desires must be sacrificed for them, and to evaluate their rela-tive values. This enables him to choose to pursue the satisfac-tion of some desires rather than others, and to realize and accept the necessity of frustration and delay. Thus, in a real sense he is the master of his desires rather than a slave to them.

He also employs the knowledge he acquires from his inter-action with his expanded environment to correct his conceptions of himself and of his world. He has a more detailed and accurate picture of what his capabilities are. He is also more aware of which of his actions and which aspects of his environment are dangerous. These, too, serve to guide his actions and to make him the master of his desires.

Ethical Evaluation

The maturing student uses a less infantile morality to evaluate his actions. He does not evaluate them merely in terms of whether they will result in praise or punishment from others. He is able to evaluate them in terms of ethical principles which he has internalized and accepted as his own. He experiences ethical evaluation of his actions not as something imposed on him from the outside, but as an autonomous process. This enables him to suppress those of his actions which would meet with censure and disapproval without feeling that he is being forced to do so. It also helps him to conceive of himself as a "good" person.

Intellectual Functioning

The maturing student has actualized much of his potential intellectual resources. He has been forced to do so in order to meet the challenges and to exploit the opportunities of his expanded environment. He has also learned especially efficient ways of using these resources in his formal education. Thus, the finiteness of his natural endowment is the only limitation on his intellectual functioning.

An Integrated Student

The student who has made the normal amount of progress in the areas mentioned above for his stage of development has taken important steps toward becoming a well-integrated and self-satisfied person. He has expanded interests and desires, the capacity to control them through reality testing and ethical evaluation, and the intellectual resources to achieve them. He is certainly ready to meet the challenges that life offers and to exploit its opportunities in the classroom or elsewhere.

THE EMOTIONALLY DISTURBED STUDENT

The students described in the three case studies differed from the ideal of the well-integrated student in many respects. A description of how they function in the areas of reality orientation, reality testing, ethical evaluation, and intellectual processes reveals both the dimensions of personality along which emotionally disturbed students differ from normal students and the varying degrees of these differences.

Reality Orientation

Ralph's reality orientation was extremely poor. When he was in school he was usually too preoccupied with his own feelings and fantasies and too anxious about his educational limitations to be truly interested in the curriculum. In fact, he was so inner-oriented that he often had to be shaken physically in order to be brought back to reality. He was also quite detached from other people. When he did relate to others, he did not do so for the purpose of emotional gratification. Instead, he sought material gratification from them and attempted to manipulate them for his own ends.

Joan was much more reality-oriented. However, she had her problems in this area, too. Her ability to remain involved with her environment was limited by her self-preoccupations. She was also more able than Ralph to relate to people. But, although she sought to develop stable, affective relationships with others, she was unable to accomplish this because of her periodic feelings of rejection. The major difference between her and Ralph was that she had developed a greater capacity for reality relationships. Her difficulty was that her problems interfered periodically with her ability to use this capacity.

Deborah had few problems in this area. She was almost always attuned to her environment and was quite capable of entering into mature, affective relationships with others. Her difficulties occurred because she was able to deny this capacity and to relate to some people solely in terms of her own material gratifications.

Reality Testing

In the area of reality testing, Ralph was again the most limited of the three students. His misperceptions of his environment were so gross that he adhered to rituals in order to avoid unreal dangers and attacked people whom he erroneously imagined were about to attack him. His self-concept was equally distorted. At times, he was so caught up with his grandiose notions of himself that he insisted that he be sent to a regular school, and acted as if his teachers should take their counsel from him. At other times, he was so convinced that his thoughts were distorted and "crazy" that he implored people not to reveal them to others.

Joan's reality testing was relatively unimpaired. She occasionally blamed herself for things she could not have done, misperceived others as unreasonably rejecting, and doubted her abilities. These misperceptions, however, were very unlike Ralph's distortions. Hers were **suspicions** which were amenable to correction through additional reality testing rather than **firm beliefs** which were resistant to reality testing.

Except in one area, Deborah's reality testing was excellent. Her appraisals of her environment, interpretations of the actions of others, evaluations of her capacities, and judgments of the results which would ensue from her actions were all usually quite accurate. Her reality testing broke down only when her desires were so overriding that she had to distort reality in order to defend herself against the anxiety and guilt these satisfactions would have produced. On these occasions her excessive use of rationalization and reaction formation left her unaware of her true feelings and motives and led her to distort those of others.

Ethical Evaluation

Although these three students had internalized sets of moral principles, all had difficulty in applying them. Ralph's ethical principles had very little effect on his behavior because the anxiety and fear which underlay his impulsive actions was often too intense to be contained by ethical considerations. In addition, his impulsive behavior usually resulted from such distorted perceptions of reality that he probably saw little, if anything, unethical about it.

Deborah's ethical principles also failed to exert much influence on her behavior. In her case this was not due to the intensity of the emotions which underlay her behavior. It was due to her successful employment of rationalization and reaction formation to defend herself against any ethical discomfort her actions might have caused her.

Joan was quite affected by her ethical principles and usually felt very guilty whenever she failed to conform to her own expectations or those of others. Unlike Deborah, who experienced her undesirable behavior as desirable aspects of her personality, Joan was quite uncomfortable about her undesirable actions. Her problem was not that she did not feel enough appropriate guilt to control her actions; it was that she often felt guilty when it was inappropriate to do so.

Intellectual Functioning

Of the three students, Ralph was the only one whose intellectual functioning was severely impaired. He had considerable difficulty with such processes as planning, organizing, conceptualizing, and reasoning. He even had difficulty with such relatively simple processes as attention, concentration, and rote memory.

Deborah's and Joan's intellectual processes were unimpaired. Their occasional problems resulted from an inability to use their capacities because of transitory states of anxiety or depression.

Summary

These comparisons indicate that emotionally disturbed students vary in the extent to which they differ from their normal counterparts. In any one area of personality some disturbed students may have severe problems and others may function normally. To the extent that the problems of these three youngsters were typical of emotionally disturbed students, the descriptions of how they function indicate that emotionally disturbed students differ from normal students in the following ways: They are usually less reality-oriented. Some are so constantly preoccupied with their own feelings and ruminations that they have little interest in the external world. They prefer their own fantasies to the companionship of others. Other emotionally disturbed students who are usually well related to their environment turn inward only periodically.

In general, they are less able to maintain stable, affective relationships with others. Those who are excessively concerned about their own gratification have apparently not developed the capacity to relate to other people except as satisfiers of their material wants. Others have developed the capacity for maintaining stable, emotional relationships but are prevented from doing so by their emotional problems.

Some students' perceptions of their world are severely distorted. They tend to misinterpret the actions and motives of others, they are plagued by unfounded fears, they have mistaken evaluations of their own capacities, and they are unable to predict the results of their actions. They accept their distortions as truths and they are very resistant to any reality testing imposed on them. Other students have only occasional breaks in reality testing. Their distortions may take the form of self-doubt and suspicion, which are more amenable to reality testing. Or they may result from overly defended self-perceptions, which are much more difficult to correct.

Some students are almost constantly beset by feelings of anxiety, guilt, and depression. They are usually unable to function effectively at these times. They resort to various objectionable, interpersonal devices to cope with their feelings and then later feel uncomfortable about the inappropriateness and undesirability of their subterfuges. They may even feel anxious and guilty when it is inappropriate to do so. Other students who have the same underlying feelings are more successful in defending themselves against them. They usually seem quite calm and emotionally stable. However, they achieve this at the cost of misperceiving their actions to the point that they are literally unaware of their true motives. Unlike the first group of students, they are quite comfortable with their objectionable behavior.

Some students' abilities to use their potential intellectual resources are severely impaired. Others can function effectively except during periods of immobilizing anxiety, preoccupying depression, or similar disturbed emotional states.

These students also vary greatly in their capacities to control their behavior. Some who are extremely intolerant of delay and frustration, or who distort their environment to the point where it becomes overwhelmingly threatening, are often quite unable to control their actions. Others who may also be somewhat intolerant of frustration and delay are usually more able to control their actions through reality testing and ethical evaluation. Still others are overcontrolled in specific areas because of excessive guilt or anxiety which would result from action.

THE EDUCATIONAL SIGNIFICANCE
OF DIAGNOSTIC CATEGORIES

An assessment of the three emotionally disturbed students in terms of the dimensions of personality discussed above offers a useful shorthand description of some of the problems of the students in the diagnostic categories which each typifies. An assessment of the students in the case studies in terms of these dimensions reveals the most significant ways in which the three major groups of emotionally disturbed students that they typify differ.

The Schizophrenic

Ralph exhibited extreme problems in all areas. He was quite inner-oriented and related to people as objects to be manipulated for his own use. His reality testing was grossly defective, and his ability to utilize his intellectual potential was severely impaired. Most important, his ability to control his actions through reality testing or ethical evaluation was enormously limited. As a result, his capacity for coping with life was quite meager. Ralph typifies the student diagnosed as a **childhood schizophrenic** who has gross impairment in all the above areas and a meager capacity to cope with life.

The Neurotic

Deborah and Joan typify two subcategories within another major diagnostic category of emotional disturbance. Both had few, if any, defects in their reality testing and intellectual functioning. Their major problems were in the areas of reality orientation, frustration tolerance, and control. But even in these areas their difficulties were less severe than Ralph's.

Joan was often in a state of emotional turmoil. When she was unable to employ unacceptable methods of satisfying her desires because of the guilt, she would feel frustrated and anxious. And yet, when she did employ these methods, she felt guilty and anxious and ashamed. Whichever alternative she chose, she remained in a state of unresolved emotional conflict.

Deborah, on the other hand, was seldom emotionally upset. She avoided frustration by getting and doing what she wanted. And she avoided guilt by misperceiving her actions. She, too, could have suffered from emotional conflicts, but she was too adept at defending herself.

A second major difference between them which was alluded to above was their subjective experience of their actions. Joan was well aware of her undesirable behavior, and she felt uncomfortable about it and wanted to get rid of it. On the other hand, Deborah so misperceived her objectionable actions that she was unaware of what she was really doing.

Joan typifies the **symptom neurotic** who experiences her objectionable behavior as discomforting symptoms. Deborah typifies the **character neurotic** whose undesirable methods of dealing with her emotional problems are integrated into her character and experienced as desirable aspects of it.

Qualifications

Since these three students represent only three of the many categories of emotional disturbance, not all emotionally disturbed students can be fitted neatly into one of these categories. Important differences even among students who obviously fall into any one particular category are always observed. Not only do such students differ in the extent to which their functioning in any one area is impaired; they also differ in the ways in which they cope with their impairments. In addition, other variables, such as age, motivation for academic success, native intellectual endowment, reaction to external influences, and family pressures, will naturally vary from student to student. Thus, fitting a student into one of these diagnostic categories does not offer a cookbook approach for understanding his educational difficulties and choosing solutions for them. It only delineates the areas in which his problems are likely to lie and some of the personality factors which may help to determine whether specific techniques offer appropriate solutions for them.

EDUCATIONAL TECHNIQUES

Dangers of Overgeneralization

Because most general suggestions about techniques for handling their more obvious educational difficulties are as likely to be wrong as they are to be right there is an ever-present danger of overgeneralization in any discussion about techniques for working with emotionally disturbed students. There are a number of reasons for this. Such educational difficulties as withdrawal, negativism, disruptiveness, provocation, cheating, and paraphrasing are inappropriate solutions for underlying problems which themselves require varying techniques. For example, the educator has to use one set of techniques to help the student who persistently refuses to answer questions in class if his refusal is an attempt to hide his distorted perceptions of the world, another group of techniques if it is the student's way of resolving his self-doubts, and a third set of techniques if the student is fighting against what he imagines to be attempts to control him. In addition, problems that superficially appear to be similar may require different techniques because of other aspects of the student's personality, for example, whether he is aware of his behavior and feels guilty about it or is overly defended against it and comfortable with it.

Even generalizing about techniques for handling the more basic problems which underlie the student's educational difficulties can be misleading. Their appropriateness also depends on additional factors, such as the availability of an interdisciplinary team. For example, since the educator is not in a position to judge how far he can go in confronting Ralph with his intellectual difficulties without precipitating the kind of self-destructive behavior which actually occurred, he will probably handle the problem in one way if the counsel of Ralph's psychotherapist was available and in another way if it was not.

In order to avoid the dangers of overgeneralization as much as possible, the suggestions included in this chapter are limited primarily to techniques for dealing with basic underlying problems. These suggestions include those which are appropriate for an interdisciplinary team approach and those which are especially appropriate when clinical services are unavailable.

The Inner-Oriented Student

The student who is preoccupied in class with irrelevant thoughts and fantasies presents problems to the teacher for two reasons: he may fail to attend to his class work because of his tendency to drift away into his own reveries; and he may act out the anxiety, guilt, shame, or elation his reveries arouse.

There are a number of measures a teacher can take in order to discourage a student from drifting off. The seating arrangements can be utilized effectively, class assignments can be made with an eye to keeping his attention, and he can be watched carefully and called upon whenever he appears to be straying.

Making the content of the curriculum, and especially the method of its presentation, as personally meaningful as possible should also help to keep him focused on the work at hand. Ingenuity and creativity in making the curriculum personally meaningful to the inner-oriented student distinguishes the teacher who captures the student's interest from the one who has to discipline him. The following example illustrates how one educator made his introduction to the topic "What Were the Causes of World War I?" meaningful to his students.

For a minute or two after the class had been seated, he said nothing. Then he asked each of them their ages and again maintained his silence. When one of the students asked why he had raised the question, he replied that he had been wondering if any of them was old enough to volunteer for the army. Soon the students' attention was focused on whether they would feel obligated to fight for their country in a third world war. Their discussion quickly turned to World War II and then to World War I. Since most of them had already agreed that they would need to determine whether a war was justified before they could decide whether they would feel duty-bound to fight for their country, they found themselves involved in the lesson prepared by the teacher. This introduction was in sharp contrast to "Class, now we are going to discuss the causes of World War I."

In spite of his best attempts, even the most skillful teacher may find at times that the student is too preoccupied with other concerns to attend to the work at hand. He may be preoccupied with his guilt feelings as Joan was when she wrote the following note to herself in class: "I want to do so many things. I want to be nice to Mr. Williams . . . I like him . . . I can't. Why won't someone hit me? Why can't I be punished?" Or he may be too elated to concentrate as Joan was when she wrote the following note to one of her friends: "I'm in a very stupid mood today, so when Mr. Williams said, 'Stop that and work along with the class,' I thought he said, 'Stop that and burp along with the class,' and it cracked me up."

When the student is too preoccupied to attend to the work at hand, trying to force him to do so would be as fruitless as ordering him to fall asleep, despite the worries which are keeping him awake. A very depressed, preoccupied student wrote the following essay during an exam which his teacher insisted that he take. The first word in each line discloses what he thought about being coerced to function when he was too depressed to do so:

> *I* feel that the Negroes actually
> *don't* want so much integration. They
> *like* to be equal, but because of their
> *problems* they push the issue of this,
> *of* inequality. They feel they are
> *American* and they are members of a
> *democracy.* This makes them fight,
> *I* believe, and their reasoning I
> *think* is fight just for principle, and
> *it's* the principle, the basic rights are
> *boring* to Negroes. The principle of
> *this* rash of demonstrations, the
> *message* they want to get across
> *is* "we are equal." Mass demonstrations
> *accidental* as it may seem throughout cities
> *end* in riots because whites want
> *the* Negroes to lose face saying
> *demonstrations* lead to riots.

Occasionally, the inner-oriented student may become so engrossed in his fantasies that he acts them out. Ralph did this when he led a band in class and when he attacked other students. The educator who is aware of a student's tendency to be affected in this way can keep a watchful eye out for the clues which often disclose that something is afoot, and often intervene before anything occurs. Even if he misses the clues, he is less perplexed by what occurs and better prepared to handle it than he would be if he were not aware of the possibility of such behavior.

The Self-Doubting Student

The educational difficulties which result from a student's self-doubts and feelings of inadequacy and inferiority were discussed at length in the case studies of Joan, Ralph, and Deborah. However, the important differences among the students, especially between Joan and Ralph, which necessitated the use of different techniques, were mentioned only in passing.

Joan's self-doubts were not so extreme that she needed to defend herself against them. Since the educator was able to relate himself to them directly because she was quite aware of them herself, he was able to reassure her about them, point out their inappropriateness, and use the various techniques described earlier to build up her self-confidence.

Ralph's self-doubts, on the other hand, were so extreme that he had to resort to a grandiose resolution of them. Since these self-doubts were not readily available to him, the educator could not deal with them directly without attacking Ralph's defenses. Moreover, he was not in a position to deprive Ralph of his defenses without the cooperation of his psychotherapist because he could not gauge how far he could go without precipitating self-destructive or other extreme actions. The extreme behavior which resulted when his teachers attacked his defenses, in spite of the availability of his psychotherapist to guide their efforts to handle Ralph's feelings, underscores the dangers of doing so without his aid. When an educator is faced with the necessity of helping, without clinical assistance, a student who has resorted to a grandiose solution to severe feelings of inadequacies, he should not tear down that student's defenses. Instead, he should concentrate his efforts on decreasing the student's need for his grandiose solution by building up his self-confidence in the ways described earlier. The way in which one teacher handled the grandiosity of a student very much like Ralph without attacking his defenses is described in the following paragraphs.

Stanley was a very well-built, eleventh-grade youngster who was intensely motivated toward academic work. Although he had above-average intellectual potential, he was barely able to function at the ninth-grade level because of a schizophrenic disorder. He always sat in the back row and refused to allow anyone to be behind him. He thought that people were talking about him and laughing at him, and he displayed his physical prowess as if to frighten off would-be attackers. His standards were perfectionistic and he was extremely sensitive to any hint of criticism. The extent of his perfectionistic standards is revealed in the following excerpt from a letter of application which he wrote for a job. The teacher had stressed that both the job for which he was applying and the summary of his qualifications should be as realistic as possible. He wrote:

> I understand that you have an opening for a secretary. I have had vast experience in all fields. I graduated from a high school for gifted students and I just finished a ten-year college course. I just received my bachelors and masters degree. I had courses in psychoanalysis and psychotherapy.
>
> I graduated from high school with a ninety-eight average. I had twenty-six credits when I left. I was an honors student for four years. I was leader of the commercial class. I was first in my physics class. I was first in my chemistry class. I was best in trigonometry . . .
>
> During the war I was selected to defend my country while I was in college. I spent four years in action. I lost my right leg. I won the Navy Cross, the Medal of Honor, the Purple Heart, the Medal of Honor, the Distinguished Service medal, and the Legion of Merit . . .

During the early weeks of the term Stanley created major disturbances and threatened to hit the teacher whenever his work was corrected or evaluated. Even on the few occasions when he received a 90 or a 95, he insisted on having a detailed account of why he had lost any "credit" at all. Whenever the teacher made such remarks as, "It is getting too noisy," or "Perhaps we ought to do this tomorrow so that more of you will be prepared," Stan rose up out of his seat, assumed a boxer's stance, glared at the teacher, and insisted on defending himself. He continued to do this although his teacher repeatedly explained that such remarks were not directed toward everyone, but only to those to whom it applied.

The educator soon realized that Stan was unable to accept any reality which was less than at least 98 percent in a school for gifted students because he needed the relief from his terrible feelings of inadequacy which his grandiosity afforded him. Since Stan could not tolerate reality testing and became anxious and disruptive whenever he was confronted with it, the educator decided to keep his reality testing to a minimum. Instead of noting all the errors in Stan's written work and oral recitation, he made note of only a few in his written work and none that Stan made orally in front of the class. He stopped assigning grades to Stan's work and wrote occasional comments on it such as "Shows effort," "Good work," and "Obvious progress."

At the same time, the teacher concentrated on enhancing Stan's self-concept to the point where he could accept additional reality testing. Fortunately, Stan was extremely well motivated and could perform quite adequately in areas where his emotional problems did not interfere with his functioning. Since Stan was especially interested in the vocabulary work which the class was doing—perhaps because using "big" words belied his feelings of inadequacy—the teacher decided to focus his efforts in this area. Unfortunately, although Stan could learn the meanings of words with ease, he often misused them because he did not understand the parts of speech. The teacher therefore began his campaign by calling on Stan to define particularly difficult words and also by tutoring him in parts of speech.

In a short while, Stan was the unacknowledged class vocabulary expert. When he had mastered the parts of speech and was earning high grades, the teacher started to grade his vocabulary work. At first he gave Stan adjective ratings, then letter grades, and, finally, numerical ones. Each time Stan was able to accept a particular grading system on his vocabulary tests, the teacher evaluated his other work in the same way. He still occasionally rebelled against his grades, but his rebellions were much milder.

At the outset of the second term, the teacher presented Stan with a dictionary, officially designated him as class vocabulary expert, and notified the students that they should direct all future queries about vocabulary to him. About one month later, the teacher's relationship with Stan had improved so dramatically and he had become so much more tolerant of evaluation that the teacher thought that Stan might be ready to laugh at his perfectionism. The next time Stan complained about his vocabulary grade, the teacher mimicked him. Stan smiled, the class smiled, and everyone laughed at the vocabulary expert who had complained about a grade of 95.

Early in May Stan scored an amazing 99 percent on a particularly difficult vocabulary test which the class had taken in preparation for their reading of a play, "The Importance of Being Earnest." The teacher sent a special letter about Stan's achievement to various staff members and placed a copy on the bulletin board. Stan never created any difficulties in class after that.

The Fearful Student

Some students become extremely upset during class when topics such as disease, mental illness, divorce, persecution, and war are broached. Their reactions can range from mild tension and restlessness to outright terror.

In an interdisciplinary team approach it may occasionally be desirable to arouse the fearful student's fears in the classroom so that he can work them out in therapy. However, even in such a setting, it is usually more desirable to avoid arousing the student's unfounded fears if possible. This would certainly be true in a school setting in which clinical services are not available.

The educator can neutralize the curriculum, that is, eliminate some of its more threatening aspects, if he is aware of the topics which are likely to be upsetting. This may be appropriate for a group of extremely disturbed schizophrenic students. But it is usually unnecessary for most students even if they are as severely disturbed as Ralph. Instead, it may be possible for the educator to reassure the student before the topic is broached by moving close to him if he appreciates closeness and making a reassuring comment. At other times, it may be necessary to allow him to miss a particular class or portion of it if the topic to be discussed is likely to be too threatening to him. Forcing him to face the topic despite his fears, in the hope of proving their irrationality to him seldom works. It usually only creates additional difficulties.

The Ethically Ineffective Student

An educator of emotionally disturbed students is often tempted to relate to their behavior in ethical rather than practical terms. He may be inclined to relieve a student of what appears to him to be excessive guilt feelings or he may want to tear down a character neurotic's defenses so that his dammed up guilt and anxiety may help to control his objectionable behavior. However, the educator treads on dangerous ground if he does so because he cannot be sure of what underlies the student's behavior.

For example, after he has relieved the student of his seemingly excessive guilt, he may find that he has not freed him from the demands of an excessively stern set of ethical principles, but rather that he has given him permission to behave impulsively. In the same way, after he has torn down the defenses of the character neurotic, he may discover that instead of freeing appropriate guilt and anxiety which is capable of keeping the student's objectionable behavior in check, he has actually unleashed a reservoir of excessive guilt and anxiety which is capable of driving the student into a state of acute anxiety or depression. For these reasons it would probably be best for the educator who works alone to avoid the ethical aspects of his students' educational difficulties and relate to them in terms of their undesirable consequences.

The Overly Defended Student

Different aspects of the relation between defenses and educational difficulties have been discussed in the three case studies and in the sections about students with inadequate self-concepts and ethical evaluation difficulties. This section includes a more thorough and organized consideration of the subject.

The educator who wishes to relate himself to the students' defenses must make two decisions about them. The first one relates to their desirability: some defenses are desirable because they keep objectionable behavior in check or lead to more adaptive behavior. For example, students may react against anxiety-evoking self-doubts by striving to succeed in school as Stan did. Such students should not be discouraged from doing so. Other defenses are undesirable. They may dam up the anxiety or guilt which might keep objectionable behavior in check as they did in Deborah's case. These, of course, should be discouraged.

The second decision which the educator must make relates to the necessity of the defenses. Although undesirable defenses should be discouraged, some may be necessary, at least for the moment. This was clearly seen in the feelings of anxiety and depression, and the self-destructive and disruptive behavior which resulted when Ralph's, Stan's, and Deborah's defenses were threatened by reality testing. Since, as we have seen above, the educator is seldom able to determine with reasonable certainty that a student's defenses are both undesirable and unnecessary, he is not usually in a position to tear them down but must try other strategies.

One very desirable technique already discussed is to decrease the overly defended student's need for some of his defenses. This can sometimes be accomplished primarily by educational means as in the case of Stan's inability to accept evaluation. In many instances it requires a total therapeutic effort to do so. This is often true with students who are unable to tolerate frustration.

Another useful way in which to work with an overly defended student is to present a clearer picture of reality to him without forcing him to perceive it if he is not ready to do so. The educator can do this by informing the student that he disagrees with his perception of reality, but without forcing his own perceptions upon him. This was substantially what Stan's teacher did when he informed Stan that he did not agree with his evaluation of his own work, and then stopped confronting him with his performance until he was ready to accept it. However, this was not the procedure followed by Deborah's and Ralph's teachers who confronted them with their misperceptions and insisted that they look at them.

Another somewhat related technique is to make it more difficult for the overly defended student to employ his defenses without preventing him from doing so if he really needs them. In the case of a student like Joan, who tends to blame others for her difficulties, this would involve structuring the situation so that it is difficult for her not to assume responsibility for her own actions. Joan's teacher always made preparations for her to take examinations elsewhere in case she suddenly found somthing at which to be angry and stormed out of the room.

Although these measures may eventually help the overly defended student, the educator is still faced with the student's defenses in the present. He needs to be able to determine whether the student is aware of his motives and actions in order to use this knowledge in determining how to react to the student's behavior. He also needs to be able to distinguish between defensive distortions and deliberate deception so that he can treat them differently.

The Misperceiving Student

The educator who knows the kinds of misperceptions a student is likely to have can prevent many of them from occurring. If he is aware that a student tends to misperceive others as arbitrarily attempting to exert their control over him, he can make his role as the authority figure less objectionable to the student by requesting and suggesting rather than by insisting and ordering. He can also avoid backing the student into a corner in which the student must either capitulate or rebel. If he knows that a student tends to misperceive people as rejecting, the teacher might establish a relationship with him in which he would be less likely to make the kinds of requests which would have to be refused. The teacher could use the techniques described earlier for dealing with students who attempt to blame others for their own difficulties. The technique used by Stan's teacher to dispel his fears of evaluation could be applied to a student who misperceives censure. Avoiding the often-used phrases of "I know you can do it" and "I told you so" would also help with such a student. Being a warm, accepting teacher with a student who anticipates hostility, and encouraging him to express his feelings and fears with impunity may do much to obviate his transference difficulties.

Unfortunately, it is not always easy to determine what the student's misperceptions are, because his inappropriate behavior may result from many different kinds of misperceptions. An educator who works within an interdisciplinary team may often be given the kind of advance information he needs. In addition, he is in a position to discuss a student's inappropriate behavior which he does not understand with the student's therapist, who can often interpret it to him. The educator who works without the aid of a clinical staff must rely primarily on his own resources. Occasionally he may be given a good psychological or psychiatric report which provides him with the kind of information he needs to cope with the student's distortions. If these are not available, anecdotal information in the school file may provide some clues. Discerning observation of the student's behavior at the outset of the term can be the basis of reasonable hypotheses about the kinds of misperceptions he has.

The following example illustrates much of what has been said about the difficulty of recognizing the student's underlying misperceptions and the necessity for doing so. It also illustrates how transference difficulties can be handled by an interdisciplinary team.

A fourteen-year-old girl who had been functioning very well suddenly began to cut classes in the middle of the term. On those few occasions when she did come, she was rather sullen and hostile—in marked contrast to her previous cheerfulness and friendliness. The teacher was completely unable to understand her behavior. He knew something was amiss, but he did not know what. About one week later he received the following letter from her:

> My Dear Mr. Smith,
>
> It has come to my attention that you have been making implications of that I have been copying Ms' homework. I feel it important to inform you that I definately do not copy *anyone's* homework. I may not hand in my

homework at the designated time but I can assure you, my dear Mr. Smith, that everything I write comes out of my brain and your textbooks.

I feel it necessary to tell you also that if you do not like me or do not wish my presence in your class you may confer with my advisor and commence with my removal from your class. Whether or not you realize it, I am young and I have a long life ahead of me and I may make up your course in any public high school after I leave.

So, Mr. Smith, I shall end my letter to you with only one thought—I like you just as little as you like me.

Sincerely yours,

B.T.

With this additional information her teacher and her therapist were able to focus her attention on the specific incident which she had originally misinterpreted. In subsequent therapy sessions her therapist helped her see in truer perspective what had actually occurred. Although her relationship with the teacher never returned to what it had been before, as a result of the intervention of the interdisciplinary team she was able to resume her place in class.

Ralph's distortions about his "crazy social studies teacher" and the "students who were about to attack him" were also dealt with effectively by an interdisciplinary approach. These examples suggest the effectiveness of such an approach, in which the educator points out the inappropriateness of the student's behavior and encourages him to discuss it with his psychotherapist, who then helps him to realize the distortions on which they are based.

The educator in a school in which an interdisciplinary team is not available cannot handle the problem in the same manner because he does not have a psychotherapeutic relationship with his students. For example, it is unlikely that Ralph would have been as able to explore his fear with the educator whom he feared, that Joan would have been able to evaluate her feelings of rejection with the educator whom she felt had rejected her, or that Deborah could have corrected her mis-perceptions of her "unfair and unfeeling" teachers by discussing her beliefs with them.

When transference difficulties arise the teacher must rely on his own efforts to correct them. The major difficulty he must overcome is the tendency of many of the student's misperceptions to become self-fulfilling prophecies because his actions often evoke the very response he had anticipated. For example, a student who anticipates hostility often brings it on himself by assaulting those who he thinks are poised to attack him. In the same way a student who anticipates rejection is likely to bring about rejection by making unreasonable demands on others, and a student who fears external control may be so quick to rebel that he requires the very control he fears.

Fortunately, the student's behavior does not always tend to evoke the kind of reaction which would confirm his misperceptions. For instance, instead of moving against others, the student who misperceives hostility may attempt to ward it off by either withdrawing from others or ingratiating himself with them. However, the educator needs to be on guard against confirming or complementing his student's misperceptions by attempting to coerce a student in rebellion against his "arbitrariness" to conform to his "reasonable expectations" without depersonalizing his actions, reacting punitively to a student's aggressive attempts to ward off his "imminent assaults," or providing the crutches which prove to the dependent student that the teacher, not the student, is the only capable one.

The Extremely Uncontrolled Student

Most emotionally disturbed students are able to control their behavior through reality testing, frustration tolerance, and ethical evaluation except when they are under severe emotional stress. However, for a small group of students, usually childhood schizophrenics, uncontrolled behavior is almost the rule rather than the exception. These students are unable to consider the implications of their actions because they are unable to delay acting long enough to contemplate them. Schooling them in the repercussions of their actions or exhorting them to behave properly has little effect on them because such lectures are forgotten in the excitement of the moment. Other measures are necessary to help these students gain control over themselves, measures which deal directly with the source of the difficulty.

Since much of their impulsive behavior is the result of their belief that if they do not receive immediate attention or gratification they will not receive it at all, keeping them well satisfied helps to assuage their need to behave in an uncontrolled manner. This can best be done in small classes in which each student receives a proportionately longer share of the teacher's attention and receives it more quickly. These students can also profit from a training schedule which instructs them that delay does not always lead to a loss, and that impulsiveness does not always lead to a gain.

Patient reminders to the child who constantly grabs for things, calls out before others have a chance, and insists upon being attended to immediately, that he will eventually receive what is due him are helpful—as long as the educator makes sure that the child does receive his due. Setting up a system of rewards which the student can earn by delaying, for example, leaving the biggest share for the last, often works wonders with such students. Such measures as ignoring answers which are called out of turn, not awarding things to the first person who grabs them, and not paying attention to the most vociferously insistent student may be among the most effective steps an educator can take.

The uncontrolled student may also cause trouble for himself and others by acting before he thinks. In industrial arts classes he is usually the one who is responsible for most of the accidents. Such a student usually responds best to extremely ordered routines which, if possible, establish a rhythmic pattern to his actions so that they become as automatic to him as tying his shoelaces. He also profits from an understanding, watchful teacher ready to intervene at the first sign of deviance from the pattern.

In general, such a student functions best in a classroom environment which discourages his uncontrolled behavior by satisfying his wants, patterning his actions, and not rewarding his impulsiveness. This environment should be flexible enough to allow for unavoidable impulsiveness, but structured enough to prevent him from harming himself and inconveniencing others. For these reasons he often needs much smaller classes than those to which most other emotionally disturbed students can adjust.

The Intellectually Inefficient Student

A student has to employ many separate mental processes in order to arrive at correct solutions for complicated problems. One mistake is often liable to lead to an erroneous solution. Most emotionally disturbed students do not have any unusual difficulty with these processes but seriously disturbed students often do. The more typical kinds of mistakes those students make are discussed in this section.

Set. A student may reach faulty conclusions because of an inability to maintain a set or stay within the framework of the problem. For example, a student was unable to multiply correctly 47×36. Each time he started with "Six times seven is forty-two, put down the two and carry the four." At this point, he was unable to resist the switch to addition which "carry the four" implied. Instead of multiplying six times four and adding four, he added six plus four plus four. Another student was unable to stick to a topic in his writing. After almost two years of drill on this problem, he began in the following way a composition in which he was supposed to describe an object without stating its use: "A thumbtack is used for many things."

Symbolic meaning. Students whose intellectual functioning is impaired by serious emotional disturbance may have difficulty with symbolic meaning because their thinking is tied to the concrete aspect of things. Such students often continue to multiply by two whenever they see the symbol for square because they cannot resist the "twoness" of it. These students are also the ones who, when they look at a map, are likely to assume that a river flows south because water flows down and south is at the bottom of the map.

Personal meanings. Some emotionally disturbed students often decide upon erroneous conclusions to problems because the problem or a part of it has personal meaning for them. For example, Stan, who was extremely suspicious that people were laughing at him and who constantly showed off his physical prowess to discourage anyone from doing so, wrote the following answer to this question: Q. Why did the American people want to expand westward in the early 1800's?" A. "When the first people came to America, the world laughed at them. We wanted to expand because we wanted to be recognized as a world power."

Another student who was also very reluctant to admit to any difficulties or problems wrote the following in answer to a question in a Problems of American Democracy course: "I love America. So I can't believe it has any problems."

Associative thinking. These students also make errors because they reach conclusions by relating two things associated together in their memory. For example, in discussing how the Crusades led to the rise of towns, one student stated, "The lords had to travel to the Italian City States to get to the Holy Land. There was a law that the lords should not be robbed. So, towns sprung up." When he was asked about his answer, he was satisfied about it because every statement was correct. However, after a discussion of his answer, he was able to see that although the statements were correct, there was no relation between the two. Another very bright student was sure that China was in Europe because "during World War II we were allied to many of the European countries and China was one of our allies." The teacher asked him if he had ever seen Chinese people and he said he had. He also knew that they belonged to the Mongoloid race, spoke an Asian tongue, and had an Asian culture. The teacher asked him if that did not suggest that China was in Asia, and not in Europe. The student thought a moment and then began to rattle off such facts as the Mongols conquered Russia and Asiatics populated Hungary. It was not until he and the teacher had looked at the map that the student agreed he had made a mistake.

Delay.   Many of these students' errors can be traced to an inability to delay judgment until they have enough evidence to arrive at valid conclusions. In the classroom they are usually the ones who, having raised their hands before the teacher has finished his questions, are unable to answer them when they are called on. They are also prone to starting work without waiting for instructions. Asking them to correct their work is usually a fruitless request because they see what they expect to see, not what they have written. Leonard, the student with superior intellectual potential who wrote the composition about the thumbtack and the answer about the Crusades, was unable to find any errors even during the third reading of the following paragraph which he had written. Each time he read the paragraph he read his errors correctly and filled in the missing words in spite of his teachers request that he examine each word carefully.

> They are eleven students in the class. Some of them are smart and so are dumb. They is one student, he name is Robert. He always talking back to the teachers. They is another students who name is Lenny. He is very smart, but he is poor in English. They are many other students.

Resistance to change.   There are many educational techniques an educator can employ to help the intellectually inefficient student overcome the difficulties which interfere with his intellectual functioning. Since techniques usually involve making the student aware of deficiencies he has successfully kept out of his awareness, they are likely to make him anxious, as if his defenses were being attacked. As a result, he is very resistant to any attempts to re-educate his intellectual functioning.

His resistance can take many forms. He can attempt to disprove his teacher, maintain that the teacher is crazy, or disrupt the class. He can become bored or try to leave the class. Finally, he can attempt to ingratiate himself with his teacher by an eagerness to please in any way short of facing his deficiencies. In short, he can move against, toward, or away from the educator. The educator who has to overcome the student's resistances without so destroying his relationship with the student that he can no longer work with him faces a difficult and trying challenge.

Overcoming intellectual ineffectiveness. There are many techniques available to the educator to help the student learn to accept delay. One social studies teacher devoted a portion of each period during the first week of the term demonstrating to his class the importance of delay of action and judgment. During the first class period, he gave them an exercise in the importance of delay, a portion of which is included below:

> This is an exercise in learning how to follow instructions. Do not write anything on this paper until you have read *all* of the instructions. Be sure to follow the directions exactly as they are given.
>
> A_____ B_____
>
> 1. Write your name in the space marked "A."
> 2. Write the date in the space marked "B."
> 3. Underline the first word in each sentence.
> 4. Circle all of the odd numbers.
> 5. Draw a line through any word beginning with the letter "L" or "N."
>   .   .   .   .   .   .
> 14. Disregard all of the above instructions except for numbers one and two.

There were many red faces when the students reached number fourteen.

On subsequent days he demonstrated the importance of delaying judgment. The class was divided into two groups. After each group had been exposed to one-sided information about a controversial topic, the students were asked to answer a set of factual questions and to state their opinions about the issue. Since all had received biased information, an argument soon arose among the students about what the facts really were. On the following day, each group was given the information the other group had received and the students were again asked to answer the questions and state their opinions. Since many of the differences among the students still persisted, the teacher was able to lead the class into a discussion of the importance of delay, the effects of previous commitments on beliefs, and the tendency of people to believe things they want to believe. These lessons did not solve the problems of the students with delay difficulties. However, they did focus their attention on these difficulties while underscoring the importance of delay in academic achievement.

Programmed instructional materials offer useful exercises in delay because they require the student to complete one task before jumping ahead to another. Other structured situations which require delayed judgment can be developed by the educator and fitted into the curriculum without difficulty.

There are also a variety of ways in which the educator can modify the curriculum in order to help the student who has difficulty with symbolic meaning, personal meanings, or associative reasoning to think more logically. He can stress cause and effect and chronological relationships in the organization of the course content. He can also introduce exercises which offer practice in the various processes which make for logical thinking. Critical evaluation of television commercials, advertisements, westerns, and historical movies offers good practice in logical thinking. Encouraging the students to correct him when he plays devil's advocate and defends a position with illogical arguments can be equally helpful. But inculcating the student with the habit of questioning his own conclusions by asking "Why?" and "Does it make sense?" is probably the most effective procedure of all.

Climate for change.   The severely disturbed student is not likely to change his thinking habits unless he is provided with an environment conducive to such change. For this reason the educator must instill in the class an acceptance of the kinds of misperceptions and misconceptions which will be brought to the surface as the student becomes more able to submit his ideas and conclusions to the test of consensual validation. He must exemplify this ideal through his own action. He should encourage the student to ask questions when he is perplexed, no matter how much he fears that they will seem stupid to others. He should also be sure to give his attention to such questions regardless of how obvious or irrelevant they may seem; otherwise the educator might not only fail to exploit an opportunity to extinguish the student's inappropriate thinking habits, but he might also convince the student that he is really not as concerned about his thinking as he says he is.

During the interim. Since these techniques do not produce immediate changes the student also needs help to succeed in spite of his difficulties. Additional guidelines, such as outlines of lectures and step-by-step descriptions of the processes involved in the various tasks which confront him, help him to maintain his set. He often requires repeated directions and periodic encouragement to check his work. Individual tutoring and close supervision of his work are also necessary. As long as his thinking remains concrete he needs examples of abstract concepts more related to his immediate life. For example, a teacher found that some students could not understand why maps were distorted until he had them eat halves of oranges and then try to flatten out the hollow peels without breaking them. This teacher also found that the following example was an aid to students who could not grasp the difference between active and passive verbs:

> When a girl returned to her college dormitory after going out with a boy on a first date, a friend asked her if she had kissed him goodnight. She replied, "No, I didn't kiss him. I was kissed by him."

Additional problems. Some of the students who have the intellectual difficulties just described, usually the younger, more seriously disturbed ones with delay difficulties, have additional problems which interfere with their ability to use their intellectual resources efficiently. They are often too hyperactive, inconsistent, disorganized, and bound to the immediate moment to be able to prepare work in advance, complete things when they are due, or work consistently on long-term projects. They even have trouble with such seemingly simple acts as bringing material back and forth to school and keeping things in their notebooks.

The educator can help these students by keeping additional

copies of books and materials on hand for them so that they are able to continue their work even when they lose, misplace, or forget to bring their work with them. In general, in spite of their good intentions, these students are ill-equipped to assume as much responsibility for their work as would be expected of other students at their age. They need other-direction to supplement their poor self-direction.

Usually, these students also have poor powers of concentration, short attention spans, and little frustration tolerance. They respond best to short-term projects, immediate reward, and a minimum of environmental distractions. Their educational achievement is increased by exposing them repeatedly to the same material through different media. It is also increased by repeated directions, an unhurried environment, and close supervision. Since even under such circumstances these students may quickly become bored or distracted, the educator needs to watch for signs of frustration, boredom, and preoccupation in order to check their problems before they become serious. Since these techniques can be employed to best advantage with small groups of students, such severely disturbed youngsters function more efficiently and attain more educational goals in small classes.

The Educationally Handicapped Student

Many emotionally disturbed students whose intellectual processes are intact have difficulty in class because the prior existence of their emotional problems has prevented them from acquiring the skills and information necessary for them to cope efficiently with the tasks appropriate for their intellectual and age levels. The educational histories of most of these students usually reveal that they had spent much too much class time daydreaming, disrupting others, visiting the principal, or playing truant, and far too little time attending to the work of the class. Some times their case histories suggest that their gaps were due to prolonged residences in institutions in which there was insufficient exposure to a wide variety of experiences.

Such a student needs a curriculum modified in ways which enable him to acquire the basic skills and information he lacks. This usually cannot be done by placing him in a group with other similar students and reviewing the essentials of a basic education because each would probably have different gaps. Such a student needs a curriculum individualized to his particular needs. There are many ways of doing this without sacrificing the benefits of education in groups. The appropriateness of each method depends primarily on the amount of time and individual attention each student's gaps require.

Deficiencies requiring only a few minutes of additional self-directed work can be handled by asking the student to review material which supplements the basic text or curriculum. Deficiencies which require more time and teacher-direction may be handled in class time set aside for such purposes. In a few areas of the curriculum, it is now possible to individualize whole units through programmed material or self-directed units designed to fill in these gaps as necessary.

EDUCATIONAL TECHNIQUE AND DIAGNOSTIC CATEGORIES

Since students in the three diagnostic categories we have been considering differ in the extent to which they are troubled by the problems just discussed, they also differ in the extent to which they require the previously mentioned educational techniques. The differences between the requirements of severely disturbed younger schizophrenic and the neurotic are especially significant. The following comments about the techniques most appropriate for different diagnostic categories are useful generalizations. However, they are subject to the qualifications and caveats necessitated by the overlap between and the variability within diagnostic categories.

The Extremely Disturbed Schizophrenic Student

The extremely disturbed schizophrenic student requires a greater number of the more extreme techniques than do the other groups. He requires almost all the modifications which were suggested for the uncontrolled student and the intellectually inefficient student. This is especially true of the younger group.

The modifications suggested for the inner-oriented, misperceiving student are also necessary. Neutralization, an extreme technique to help the fearful student, may also be required for effective educational functioning.

The Less Severely Disturbed Schizophrenic Student

The schizophrenic student who is less severely disturbed does not require as many extreme techniques because his problems are somewhat less serious. Techniques for helping him to overcome his intellectual ineffectiveness are vitally important to his educational success. The techniques for helping the inner-oriented, self-doubting, and misperceiving student are also very necessary for him. Fortunately, he is less likely to need many of the modifications suggested for the disorganized, hyperactive, and distractible student, the uncontrolled student, and the fearful student. When he does require these techniques, the less extreme ones often suffice.

The Neurotic Student

The neurotic student, regardless of the subcategory into which he falls, seldom if ever needs the curriculum modifications necessitated by severely impaired thinking processes. Nor is he likely to require the techniques appropriate for the uncontrolled or fearful student.

The symptom neurotic's major underlying difficulties are usually confined to those discussed in the sections on the misperceiving, self-doubting, and inner-oriented students. The comments made about the ethically ineffective student are also appropriate for him. The character neurotic shares most of the problems of the symptom neurotic. However, he differs from the symptom neurotic in two respects. The comments made about the overly defended student are applicable to him and those made about the self-doubting student are often not.

INDIVIDUALIZING EDUCATIONAL DECISIONS

The preceding discussions about educational techniques indicate that few educational prescriptions are appropriate for all emotionally disturbed students. How, then, can the educator arrive at decisions about such basic concerns as desirable teacher-pupil relationships, curriculum, class size, and grouping which are appropriate for a specific emotionally disturbed student? In this section we will examine how an assessment of the student in terms of the previously mentioned dimensions of personality can supply him with much of the information he requires to make such individualized decisions.

TEACHER-PUPIL RELATIONSHIPS

Although most of what has been written about desirable relationships between teachers and normal pupils would apply to the relationship between teachers and emotionally disturbed students, certain aspects of the relationship would vary with the student's underlying problems. Unfortunately, it is extremely difficult to assign different kinds of relationships to specific underlying problems because the relationship one problem requires is often the opposite of that required by another one. For this reason the following comments should be read with the proviso "unless contraindicated by other factors."

Pressure for Conformity

One of the basic questions an educator must answer about his relationship with his student is how much pressure for conformity the student should be given. The general solution suggested in the analysis of the case studies is that the educator should tolerate as much deviant behavior as necessary while demanding as much appropriate behavior as possible. The optimum balance between tolerance of deviancy and pressure for conformity is dependent on the amount of objectionable behavior which cannot be avoided because it is either beyond the student's control or temporarily expedient. Ralph's fearful responses to the topic of disease and Stan's compelling desire to sit in the last row were examples of relatively uncontrolled behavior which required a permissive reaction rather than pressure for conformity from the teacher. Stan's resistance to evaluation required a similar response because his grandiose solution to his intense feelings of inferiority was a temporary necessity. Pressure for conformity may also have to be relaxed periodically for such students as Joan whose ability to accept external direction is limited by their concern about external control and dominance.

Structure

A second decision, one somewhat related to the previous one, is concerned with the structure to which the student is expected to conform. This time the question to be answered is how well defined, consistent, and other-directed the classroom structure should be. Again the answer depends on the personality of the individual student. Many students may not require any extra structure. Very impulsive, uncontrolled students, disorganized students, and easily distracted students require a great deal of extra structure. However, even these students may profit from a tolerant response to their unavoidable departures from the extra structure imposed on them.

Emotional Closeness

In general, emotional closeness is a desirable factor in the teacher-pupil relationships. However, emotionally disturbed students vary in the amount of such closeness they can accept. Some students, especially those who are extremely fearful or suspicious of others and those who are beset with concerns about being controlled or used by others, require relatively distant relationships with their teachers until they can tolerate closer ones. Sexually seductive students may also have to be kept at an emotional distance by their teachers. Otherwise, the educator can unwittingly foster a one-sided love affair in the imagination of the student which may prevent the latter from attending to the work at hand or even lead to undesirable, poorly disguised sexual advances toward him.

Other students, especially the very fearful ones who welcome the emotional support of adults and the students who need to be assured of immediate attention and gratification, respond better to a very close relationship with their teachers. They often need such relationships until they can tolerate more emotional independence.

CURRICULUM

The curriculum requirements of emotionally disturbed students are extremely varied. Some of them do not require modifications of either the content of the course of study or the method of its presentation because they are able to function effectively. The modifications necessary for other students may make the course too elementary, repetitive, and boring for them. Deborah was an example of such a student.

The educationally handicapped student may require only such minor changes in the curriculum as an initial emphasis on basic skills until his educational gaps are filled. A student with considerable impairment in his intellectual functioning needs the major changes in both content and method mentioned above to help improve his problem-solving abilities.

The extremely disorganized, hyperactive, distractible student may require modifications which depart even more radically from the traditional content and method. The very fearful student requires a neutralized content which is inappropriate for most students who can tolerate many of the themes which upset him.

CLASS SIZE

The optimum class size for any student depends on his underlying problems. Uncontrolled students, students who desire a great deal of personal attention and immediate gratification, and students with severe impairment of their intellectual functioning usually require a considerable amount of individual attention from their teachers. For this reason they require much smaller classes than the classes to which many other emotionally disturbed students can adjust. The most seriously disturbed students in this group may almost require their own teacher or own cubicle for much of their class time.

Many emotionally disturbed students who do not have these problems and can perform as well as Joan or Deborah may be able to adjust to a class of twelve or more and still obtain as much individual attention as they need.

Students who require a distant, impersonal relationship with their teacher, such as students rebelling against external dominance, students who are afraid of imminent attack by adults, and students who need to withdraw periodically because of depression and anxiety may function better initially in a larger group because it offers them the needed opportunity for insulation.

GROUPING

Many emotionally disturbed students can tolerate any reasonable grouping. Placing them into peer group classes in which there is sufficient homogeneity so that they can all use substantially similiar material, work on similar tasks, and adhere to fairly similar management procedures is all that is required. However, some of them do have difficulties which can be exacerbated by certain kinds of grouping.

A few students have problems which make their adjustment to heterosexual groups a difficult one. Deborah's reaction to the entrance of the boys into the class was a mild example of this. A much more difficult problem for the educator was the young girl who became panicky whenever a male approached her because she was afraid he was going to rape her. Some well-defended students are threatened when their placement in a group attacks their defenses. The grandiose student may react quite negatively to being placed in a group of "idiots" who are functioning at his level. A student who has assumed a delinquent façade may feel equally threatened by placement in a class of fairly compliant students whom he sees as a "bunch of babies," "mama's boys," or "bushes," as they are called in the present-day vernacular. Other problems are also exacerbated by specific groupings.

Occasionally, placement of a student in a group within which he would be able to function is contraindicated by the group's inability to tolerate his deviant behavior: overt homosexuality, extreme aggressiveness, and bizarre, ritualistic behavior are some of the problems which are likely to upset groups. However, as stated earlier, these problems are exceptions rather than the rule.

When such problems are anticipated, the educator may decide that an alternate placement is advisable in order to minimize the problems which might limit the students' educational achievement. Or he may decide to proceed with the placement in order to provide them with an opportunity to work through their problems. The difference between the two approaches is discussed in the following section.

EDUCATIONAL TECHNIQUE WITH THE INTERDISCIPLINARY TEAM

The relationship between educational technique and the interdisciplinary team has already been dealt with to some degree in various sections of this book. This relationship is examined in a more organized and comprehensive manner in this section.

The interdisciplinary team can further the educator's efforts to achieve educational goals in many ways. One of the basic ones is providing the educator with information which is difficult for him to obtain by his own efforts. Psychological reports contain information about the existence and extent of any impairment in a student's intellectual processes and are a valuable aid in planning a student's educational program. The interdisciplinary team is able to furnish the educator with insights into the student's motivational dynamics, such as his areas of conflict, transferences, fears, and self-concept. This enables him not only to understand his students' classroom problems when they occur, but also to anticipate and thereby avoid many of them. The team can also supply information which helps him handle difficulties when they do arise: whether the student has defended himself against an awareness of his motives and actions, how necessary his defenses are, the extent to which he can control his behavior, the kinds of teacher-pupil relationships which would be most effective in bringing about changes in the student's behavior, and so on.

The team also furthers the educator's efforts by helping the student with problems which interfere with his educational functioning. For example, a therapist can help a student to become more aware of what he is doing and the way in which he contributes to his own difficulties. He can also clear up many of the student's transferences. He is in a better position to deal with the emotions which interfere with the student's educational progress and to supply the student with the kind of gratification and attention he needs in order to eliminate some of the pressing desires which underlie some of his classroom difficulties.

EDUCATIONAL TECHNIQUE WITHOUT THE INTERDISCIPLINARY TEAM

In general, the educator who works without the benefits of the interdisciplinary team has less insight into his students' motivational dynamics, less knowledge about how their problems should be handled, and little, if any, psychotherapeutic intervention in problems which require it. This limits his ability to cope with his students' problems in a number of ways.

He is relatively unable to determine with reasonable certainty which of his students' defenses are desirable or unnecessary and he is also in a poor position to assuage the intense anxiety or depression which a premature confrontation might arouse. Therefore, he must of necessity avoid direct attacks on his students' defenses. For somewhat analogous reasons he ought to avoid relating himself to his students' guilt. Since he is less able than a psychotherapist to handle his students' emotional upsets, he may have to demand more conformity and be less permissive in order to discourage events which would be emotionally upsetting to them. For the same reason he might have to neutralize the curriculum to a greater extent and limit his efforts to helping students, such as the delinquent who refuses to remain in the same classes with the "bushes," to work through their problems in class. Since he must rely on his own efforts to correct the students' transferences, inaccurate self-concepts, and unfounded fears, he will probably have considerably more difficulty with students with these problems as well.

EDUCATION AND THERAPY

The educator supplements the efforts of the psychotherapist in many ways. He provides information about the student's functioning in the real world of school. This information is often extremely necessary because the student's tendency to misperceive his behavior and accomplishments color his reports. When the therapist feels that a student is ready to work through a problem, the educator cooperates with him by confronting the student with measured amounts of reality. He provides a permissive atmosphere which encourages many of the student's repressed feelings and fantasies to come to the surface so that they are available for psychotherapeutic handling. Finally, he maintains a semiprotective, semireal environment in the classroom within which the student can use his peers' and his teacher's reactions to reality-test the new forms of behavior suggested by psychotherapeutic insights without suffering unnecessarily if the new forms of behavior are also inappropriate.

A successful educational experience is therapeutic in itself. The emotionally disturbed student who has experienced educational success, perhaps for the first time, probably has considerably more self-esteem because of the experience. He is also likely to have acquired a more realistic appraisal of his own abilities. A successful school experience can broaden his interests by introducing him to new aspects of his world and providing him with the additional educational and interpersonal skills he needs to meet more challenges. In order to have succeeded, he has had to learn to cease surrendering to his whims and fantasies and to sacrifice some of his less important desires for more important goals. These are some of the ways in which a successful educational experience helps to make a student a more integrated person.

THE PROBLEMS OF THE EDUCATOR

An educator who works with emotionally disturbed students has an extremely challenging job. He must remedy their intellectual difficulties and educational handicaps, assuage their anxieties and fears, and prove false their suspicions and distortions. In addition, he must be able to overcome the defenses and interpersonal techniques with which they resist his efforts to change them. With such a formidable array of obstacles in his path, any educator is bound to have difficulties. These difficulties usually occur when the students' behavior exacerbates the educator's own interpersonal problems. For when this happens, the educator's reactions to his students' emotional problems are affected by his need to cope with his own emotional discomfort.

Educators vary in terms of the kinds of interpersonal situations which are apt to be troublesome for them. The educator who is insecure about his ability to control his class and maintain his role as class authority is apt to be alert to any challenge to his position. He is likely to personalize the rebellious student's actions when the student is actually unable to conform and to misperceive students who are unable to function as unwilling to do so. When this occurs, his reactions are usually appropriate for his misperceptions of the student's behavior, but inappropriate in terms of the actual dynamics of it. Mr. Roth's and Mr. Williams' initial responses to the onset of Deborah's undesirable behavior were apparently influenced by such misperceptions.

An educator who is overly concerned about earning respect and approval and avoiding criticism or censure may allow his sensitivity in these areas to interfere in his relationships with his students. He may personalize his students' actions when they are bored and restless or when they interrupt him as signs of disrespect and respond inappropriately to their problems. He may also misperceive his students' suggestions for improving his educational techniques as criticism and be unable to profit from them.

An educator who is excessively uncomfortable with his assertive and hostile impulses may be overly susceptible to his students' claims that he is punitive or arbitrary. This can interfere with his ability to maintain consistent limits when these are required. When an educator has this problem his class is often characterized by a general, overly permissive enforcement of limits which is interrupted by episodes of stern enforcement when the students have deviated so far that he no longer feels uncomfortable about asserting himself.

The pleasure an educator receives from helping his students can cause him difficulty. It may blind him to the inappropriateness of some of his students' requests for assistance and lead him to provide them with so much of it that they do not have to face and overcome their difficulties. His desire to help his students can also cause him to underestimate unwittingly the contributions of the other members of the interdisciplinary team. It makes him susceptible to his students' efforts to persuade him to intercede with other staff members who are causing them necessary pain. Mr. Roth's willingness to treat Joan's minor lacerations and his initially sympathetic ear for her "problems" may have reflected this kind of difficulty.

If he has unresolved problems in the same area an educator may have difficulty coping with aspects of his students' personalities even if they do not affect him directly. He may misperceive some of his students' undesirable actions as desirable ones and encourage them. For example, he may encourage minor transgressions of rules, excessive self-assertiveness in peer relationships, and symbolic heterosexual conquests as signs of healthy self-assertiveness.

On the other hand, he may so overreact to certain forms of behavior which he finds intolerable because of his own problems that he is unable to handle them objectively. He may become frustrated with passive students who ingratiate themselves with their peers and allow themselves to be used as scapegoats or he may feel vehemently antagonistic toward aggressive students who push others aside and do the scapegoating. He may have difficulty accepting some students' low levels of aspiration because of his own feelings about achievement. He may also be unable to cope with students who are sexually seductive with their peers or who flaunt their imagined sexual charms in front of each other. Almost any form of behavior is capable of arousing unresolved problems in some educators.

Fortunately, there are numerous signs which can alert an educator to the fact that his own problems are impeding his efforts to help his students. His problems may be interfering when any of the following situations exist:

1. He has similar difficulties with many students.

2. Other educators have significantly different experiences with particular students.

3. He treats relatively minor matters as major concerns.

4. He believes that a student's actions reflect a desire to evoke a reaction from him rather than a poor solution to an emotional problem.

5. He finds that he is unusually hostile, solicitous, or indifferent toward a student.

6. He finds that he has less than his usual amount of control over his actions with a particular student.

Perhaps the best method he can employ to determine whether his own problems are interfering in his relationships with his students is to explore the possibility with another person who can evaluate the situation more objectively than he.

RECOMMENDED READINGS

Jersild's *Child Psychology* (1960) contains excellent chapters about fears, anxiety, and moral development in childhood.

Piaget has made important contributions to the understanding of the normal development of intelligence in his *The Origins of In-*

telligence in Children (1952). Insights into impaired intellectual functioning are contained in Freud's *The Psychopathology of Everyday Life* (1914), Goldstein and Scheerer's "Abstract and Concrete Behavior: An Experimental Study with Special Tests" (1941), and Rapaport's *Organization and Pathology of Thought* (1951).

For discussion of various symptom patterns found in emotionally disturbed students see Berkowitz and Rothman's *The Disturbed Child* (1960). Goldfarb's *Childhood Schizophrenia* (1961) describes his research with childhood schizophrenic children which suggests that there are two major groups of such children which differ in terms of the etiology and the severity of their problems.

"Changing the Delinquent's Concept of School" (1959) by Goldsmith, Krohn, Ochroch, and Kagan describes an educational approach to emotionally disturbed students who do not have gross impairment of their intellectual functioning. Newman's "The Acting Out Boy" (1956) discusses the educational needs of extremely impulsive students.

The curriculum requirements of extremely fearful students are considered by Jacobson and Falgre in "Neutralization: A Tool for the Teacher of Disturbed Children" (1959). Fenichel details an educational program for young schizophrenic children in "An Elementary School for Seriously Disturbed Children" (1953).

For contrasting views about structure and permissiveness, compare Berkowitz and Rothman's *The Disturbed Child* (1960), Bettelheim's *Love Is Not Enough* (1949), and Neill's *Summerhill: A Radical Approach to Child Rearing* (1960) with Cruickshank, Bentzen, Tannhauser, and Ratzeburg's *A Teaching Method for Brain-Injured and Hyperactive Children* (1961), Goldsmith, Krohn, Ochroch, and Kagan's "Changing the Delinquent's Concept of School" (1959), and Haring and Phillip's *Educating Emotionally Disturbed Children* (1962).

Various aspects of classroom management are considered in Redl and Wineman's *The Aggressive Child* (1957) and Cutts and Moseley, *Teaching the Disorderly Pupil in Elementary and Secondary School* (1957).

The differences between educational and psychotherapeutic approaches to emotional problems are considered by Hirschberg in "The Role of Education in the Treatment of Emotionally Disturbed Children through Planned Ego Development" (1953) and by Devereux in his *Therapeutic Education* (1956). An interdisciplinary approach to the education of emotionally disturbed students is outlined by Rabinow in "The Role of the School in Residential Treatment" (1955) and by Goldsmith, Schulman, and Grossbard in "Integrating Clinical Processes with Planned Living Experiences" (1959).

Berkowitz and Rothman, *The Disturbed Child* (1960) and Haring and Phillips, *Educating Emotionally Disturbed Children* (1962) offer somewhat contrasting conclusions about the effectiveness of certain educational techniques in a non-interdisciplinary setting.

Menninger's chapter on countertransference in his *Theory of Psychoanalytic Technique* (1961) offers insights into the way in which an educator's problems can interfere with his handling of his students' difficulties.

An Elementary Textbook of Psychoanalysis (1955) by Brenner, *An Outline of Psychoanalysis* (1949) by Freud, *Emotional Disorders of Children* (1949) and *Psychoanalysis and the Education of the Child* (1954) by Pearson, *The Psychology of Adjustment* by Shaffer and Shoben, and *The Abnormal Personality* (1964) by White all have general relevancy for the ideas considered in this book.

chapter 7

Application

ISAAC

This final case study is of a youngster who spent four years at the institution. Enough case study material is presented so that the reader can study the ways in which his behavior changed during this four-year period. No analysis of the case study is presented. Instead, the reader is encouraged to analyze the material himself. In addition to the analysis, questions are raised about the case study which highlight some of the major ideas considered in the text.

I

BACKGROUND INFORMATION

Intake Summary

Isaac is being referred to the institution because of his impulsive, violent, provocative, nonconforming behavior, and his imminent expulsion from school. He is restless, hyperactive, and demanding. He has violent temper tantrums and behaves in a manner dangerous to himself.

He is the only child of a very disturbed family. The mother is an extremely disturbed woman who has suffered several acute depressive episodes. She is disorganized, a poor housekeeper, and an anxious, overinvolved mother. The father is an immature, dependent man who is tied very closely to his own parents. There has been a good deal of marital conflict in the past three years which has resulted in a number of separations. At one point, the father removed the household furnishings. During this time, Isaac has been shunted back and forth between his parents and grandparents, and has been the center of conflict between the parents about his custody and allegiance.

Interview with the father. Isaac's father is a rather weak, immature man who seemed on the verge of tears during the interview. He stated that he has been separated from his wife for about a year. He complained about his poor marital and home life and seemed to place the entire blame on his wife. His complaints focused on a number of areas. She ran the home in a haphazard manner, seldom had his meals ready for him when he returned from work, and stayed up so late reading and listening to the radio that she was unable to wake up in time to feed Isaac and get him to school. He felt she was a poor mother because she always gave in to Isaac, allowed him to control her with his threats and tantrums, and interfered whenever he tried to discipline the boy. He was especially concerned about the way he felt she abused Isaac when she herself was upset. He stated that she often hit the boy with forks and other things when he would not eat and even sat on him. The father reported that he was losing control over Isaac because his wife had taught Isaac to hate him.

He mentioned that on several occasions she had dumped Isaac at his home or at his place of employment at any time of the day or night. On one occasion, when he attempted to return the boy to her, she locked the apartment and pretended that she was not in. When he climbed in through a window, he saw her run out into the hall. On another occasion, she left

Isaac with him because he had the measles and she did not wish to care for him.

He stated that he was an easygoing fellow and married his "fat, sloppy, and overweight" wife with a promise from her family that they would give him money. He maintained that even though they had not kept their promise, he would have been satisfied if she had been a good mother and housekeeper. He was against placement for the boy and hoped that the court would force his wife to become a good mother and housekeeper.

Interview with the mother.   During the interview she vacillated between moments of elation and bursts of tears. She stated that Isaac presented serious problems at home which she attributed to his unstable home life. She attributed the marital difficulties to her husband: he was immature, overly attached to his mother, and tense and irritable because of recurrent migraine headaches. She believed that he wanted her as a housekeeper and maid rather than as a wife and companion. She felt that he often did not keep his promise to Isaac and related an incident in which, when she put Isaac on the phone to talk with him, he pretended that there was not a person by his name at the hotel where he was staying. She cited such incidents as the reason why Isaac did not trust him.

She appeared to be quite disturbed and rejecting. Although she attempted to bring Isaac up to adhere to a strict religious code, she had been very inconsistent in her demands. She admitted that Isaac often struck both of them, was often uncontrollable, and that he needed help. However, she did not want him to be treated away from home.

Information about Isaac.   Isaac is a slim, short, twelve-year-old youngster who is unable to control his actions once he has begun anything. He has pulled emergency cords in subways, interfered with persons driving cars, and run in front of automobiles. At home he was restless and demanding. He controlled his parents with temper tantrums and often struck them physically. He seems to lack any clear image of what he is like as a person. He is unaware of his own personal needs and acts on those of his mother.

He seems to be the product of unstable parents who have used him to act out their own conflicts with each other. Without regard for him they have had numerous arguments in front of him in which they cursed and struck each other. They have also literally "dumped" him on each other whenever he was sick. In order to protect himself against his fear of losing his mother's affection, he has had to remain emotionally tied to her to the point that he has lost his identity.

Hospital report about pre-admission observation

When Isaac was first admitted to the hospital he was able to adjust to the routine. He ate his meals, bathed, and adhered to his religious codes without any conflict with the hospital routine. When his mother interfered, his behavior changed and he came into conflict with the staff. He refused to eat what was given to him and declined food for twenty-four hours when she expressed concern about his diet. He refused to bathe when she told him not to bathe because she would take him home each weekend and bathe him. When he expressed his fears about the hospital to her, she promised to take him from the hospital to the court, and she assured him that the court would send him home.

Psychological testing

Isaac literally whirled around the room while the test was being administered. Although he had been in the room only ten minutes and had met the examiner for the first time, he wanted to know if she would buy him a birthday present. Throughout the test he jumped up and down in his seat and continually asked whether his responses were correct or not. He insisted on doing other tests rather than the one on which he was working. He picked up things from the examiner's desk, opened test material, and was in perpetual motion. He seemed particularly anxious about being timed and worked with one eye on the test and the other on the watch.

He was insistent on being as irritating as possible. At one point, his behavior was so disruptive that the testing was stopped and he was asked if he wanted to continue. He insisted that he did and sat down again. However, in a few minutes he was repeating his former behavior. He tended to plunge into tasks before he fully understood what was required of him. He was quite reluctant to work on problems involving reading and asked for other tasks instead. He grew increasingly argumentative and willful as time went on. To a limited degree, he responded to urging, but increasingly would try to shift to another test or simply announced that he was not going to work any more. He paid no attention to the other boys present until he wanted them to spell a word which the examiner declined to spell. Later, ignoring the other boys' needs completely, he turned out the light because it was too bright for him.

Isaac is a youngster with almost no self-image. This was seen most dramatically when he was unable to draw a picture of himself. He is extremely anxious and unable to cope with environmental demands, despite his eagerness, as shown in repeated attempts to do so. When his attempts fail, he reacts aggressively to his frustrations.

His interpersonal relationships are dominated by his desire and attempts to obtain direction and support. When this is not forthcoming from others, he is overwhelmed by anxiety.

Tests indicated that although Isaac's native ability is in the superior range, he cannot use it because of his emotional problems. At times he lost contact with the examiner and responded inappropriately. However, when he was in contact, he performed satisfactorily. The two most salient features of the test results were the extent to which he missed easier items and passed difficult ones, and his extremely inadequate functioning on tests of social judgment and "common sense."

In general, the tests indicate that he is currently functioning within the average range of intellectual ability and can handle academic material only at the fourth-grade level.

School Functioning

Isaac was on the verge of being expelled from school because of his behavior. He missed forty-one of the ninety school days. His work was unsatisfactory.

II

ELEMENTARY SCHOOL PROGRAM
FIRST YEAR: AGE 12

Initial Psychiatric Interview

Isaac spent most of the time describing some of his more provocative escapades. He especially enjoyed relating incidents in which he provoked his mother and his eyes brightened when he told me about the scoldings he had received from her because of them. He also enjoyed telling me about motion pictures filled with violence and death. When he was insecure or suspicious of me during the interview, he attempted to seize control of the situation from me by such comments as "Okay, continue," "What's next?" and so on.

Isaac appears to be an extremely impulsive and infantile youngster whose difficulty understanding the reality about him leads to inappropriate behavior. He continues to employ the provocative and demanding approach necessitated by his relationship with his parents to obtain support from others. There are indications that he also uses this approach to gain external support when he is on the verge of losing control over his impulses. In addition, since he feels hostile about being controlled by and dependent on others, this approach also serves as an avenue for the expression of his hostility.

In order to change his behavior patterns, it will be necessary for our staff members to accept his hostility and not react with their own. He must also be confronted with very structured situations which he cannot manipulate.

Teacher's Report (Male)

Initial report. Isaac is quite childish and often giggles when the class is supposed to be quiet. He likes to annoy the other children. For example, when a pupil who had assembled a construction set left the room to go to the toilet, Isaac stripped the construction set and hid it in one of the desks.

The boy returned and became upset about it. I spoke to Isaac about this and he apologized to me for his actions. He gives the answers to blackboard work before the student who has been called upon to recite has a chance to do so. He is friendly toward me and very willing to do things for me. His work in spelling and arithmetic is good. He is very much interested in his schoolwork and often asks me for individual help. He likes to read books and work with construction sets.

Comments on his report card. Isaac should try not to annoy the other children. He should try to have more self-control and not call out answers during class.

Final report. At the beginning of the term Isaac frequently teased the other children. He does not do this as much now and is accepted by his classmates. His relationship with me is good. He accepts responsibilities such as going on errands, cleaning the room, and distributing pencils.

Progress Meeting: At the close of the academic year

Psychotherapy report. Isaac arrived at the institution during the less-structured summer program. It was almost impossible to contain him during the more permissive recreation periods. He could not follow regulations without constant external controls, he yielded to his every impulse, and often left the group. However, during this period he responded well to the structure and firmness of cottage life.

With the onset of the school program his behavior changed markedly. The structure and firmness with which he was handled in school enabled him to adjust to demands and to remain in the program.

At present, he derives a great deal of pleasure from hurting other children through constant teasing and he is quite aware of this. He also enjoys provoking fights which remind him of the times when his parents used to argue. He wants to have me all for himself, and gets angry and hurt whenever he sees me with other children. He often sits outside my office window, teasing the child I am interviewing or trying to monopolize my attention. Although he has learned to restrain his impulses, he still seems to operate on the basis of infantile needs. He is very reluctant to discuss himself.

Cottage report. He does not fight openly, but does underhanded things to make other children fight. He is very much attached to his mother. He only tolerates his cottage parents and often provokes them. After each home visit, he is more morose and disruptive. He is known as the cottage instigator. His cottage parent sees no improvement in thirteen months. Isaac does not work unless he wants to, preferring to read books. He has no friends. He adheres strictly to religious rules, but ignores cottage rules. His mother also ignores the rules and tries to get the institution to acquiesce in her wishes.

He uses his religious orthodoxy to avoid work. He says that he cannot work on the Sabbath and refuses to make up his work assignments on other days. Since his mother has not been explicit about how he should observe the Sabbath, the cottage parents are unable to deal with his religious protests.

His mother has sent numerous letters to state officials and others in an attempt to have them convince the institution to acquiesce in her wishes. These letters were quite derogatory with respect to the institution.

Psychologist's report. Isaac was almost impossible to test because of his extreme anxiety, impulsiveness, and hyperactivity. The psychological picture he presents is consistent with the one reported prior to his admission.

SECOND YEAR: AGE 13

Teacher's Report (Another Male)

Initial report. Isaac is one of the weaker boys in the group and stays out of trouble most of the time. However, he likes to tease and provoke the other children when he feels he can get away with it. He merely sticks out his tongue and thus gets several boys to blow up in rage. He likes to play stupid. This also gets the other boys upset to the point when he gets a clobbering now and then. He tries this "playing dumb" technique on adults to get them to do his work or to accept lower standards for him. When I insist on a high level of performance and do not let him pull me into his trap, he produces. He is working well in the craft program, learning and improving in all areas. He is not very skillful with his hands but he is capable of doing a decent job. Today I noticed Arnie working on Isaac's lamp. I told him not to help Isaac, but to let him do it himself. When Arnie stopped, Isaac took it up from there and did well. If I had not stopped Arnie, he would have done all the work for Isaac.

Mid-year report. Isaac is a hard-working, interested student. He has made important gains in all areas. This is especially noticeable in the craft program, where each completed project adds evidence to the fact that he is not as inept as he makes himself out to be. I have continued to face him with the fact that his clumsiness is only a mask he wears to get others to do things for him. Lately he has been getting along well with the other students in the class.

Final report. Isaac is no longer the overly conforming boy who always did as he was asked, deferred to everyone else, and was fearful of having convictions of his own. Now he can carry out a decent project by himself without having me or anyone else do it for him. Now he can tackle fractions and tell me when he does not understand without looking guilty about it. Now he can be giddy, laugh, and cut up, knowing that he is beginning to grow up. This victory came hard and not without a struggle. I told Isaac that because I would hurt him if I let him pretend he was inept, I was going to persist in proving to him and letting him prove to himself that he was capable. As a result, the need which drove Isaac to be an angel in order to please me decreased and, for a period of months, Isaac and I went through a daily struggle. He finally realized that I would not surrender to his destroying himself and he gave in.

He gets along better with the others in the class and is doing well in every area. He is only one year behind in reading and math.

Progress Report

Psychotherapist. At the outset of the year, Isaac hesitated to discuss himself, and I continually had to use games and other forms of nonverbal treatment. Then he began to use me as a link to his parents because I was seeing them regularly and he was not. About two months ago, he began to share his private world with me. His two dominant fantasies were concerned with violence and what it would be like to live with his parents. He still assumes a mask of extreme helplessness and stupidity in our sessions.

Cottage report. Isaac had very poor relations with his cottage parents because his mother undermined their authority with him during her visits. He was quite withdrawn much of the time and had to be actively drawn into the stream of cottage life. He had very few friends and spent much of his time reading books. His recent cottage change has brought about significant improvement in his cottage relationships.

Psychological Report

Behavior. In contrast to the behavior described by a previous examiner, Isaac was very serious and subdued. He was especially careful on the drawings and made constant erasures. He volunteered to tell me when he was becoming restless so that this would not interfere with the tests. He was critical of what he was doing and constantly asked for assurance from me that he was doing the right thing. He took a teasing attitude as a way of discharging tension and did his best to hold himself in severe physical restraint in order to do well.

Analysis of results. The basic problem for Isaac as revealed by psychological tests is to find safe and acceptable kinds of behavior and ideas and to use them to control his own inner, bizarre, private turbulent world. Very little of his real feelings are invested in the environment and in social relationships. A great deal of his total intellectual and emotional energy is used to control his inner, private world, to bolster up his weak sense of reality, and to keep his impulses in check. The pressure to act impulsively is still ever-present. Unfortunately, he appears to be especially sensitive to environmental excitation. He knows the difference between his own impulses and the right things to do, but when he is excited, he is unable to utilize this knowledge.

When pressure creates too much anxiety, he just goes. At these times, the combination of physical impulsiveness and emerging ideas drives him on until the storm runs its course. Explosions are still likely and the only alternative is withdrawal into a confused, whirling world of his own. When this youngster is in control of himself, he allows only a passive expression of his feelings. He becomes hyperactive at these times because of the pressure of his inner feelings and ideas.

He is a grossly infantile youngster with only a minimal sense of his own identity. Part of his struggle to find himself is reflected in his fluctuating ideas about the kind of person he is. These range from the omnipotent and grandiose to severe feelings of nothingness.

He has a confused picture of people and their roles. His world is full of menacing figures, peering faces, and nameless terrors. He sees out-and-out aggressive conflict as the only relationship that can exist between human beings.

Although Isaac received only bright-normal intelligence ratings on the test, he actually possesses superior ability. His reduced functioning is due to concentration difficulties and poor perception of reality. He has a peculiar and arbitrary way of perceiving even ordinary objects for which he has to correct. He may arbitrarily call the same thing by different names and not know he has done so. He also tends to jump to sweeping conclusions from inconsequential material. Peculiarly enough, Isaac does better under emotional pressure — provided it does not create anxiety — than he does even in a neutral situation.

Educational implications. Because of his poor sense of reality, his tendency to private thinking, his physical hyperactivity, and his difficulty in concentrating, it is doubtful that Isaac can utilize his superior abilities in school. However, he is quite capable of learning. He needs short-term and diversified activity, and special explanations and demonstrations of how ideas go together. He will also have to check his own thought processes and conclusions, especially his ideas of cause and effect, in order to make sure that he draws the right conclusions from the facts. Unless his inner pressures are relieved, it is doubtful that he will be able to achieve adequately in school because such a large proportion of his intellectual energy has been channeled into maintaining his controls. Therefore, future school planning should be kept to minimal or, at best, average goals.

THIRD YEAR: AGE 14

Teacher's Report (Female)

Initial report. At times Isaac is quite anxious in class. The past few weeks were especially anxious ones for him. He was very hyperactive, restless, and unable to contain himself. He withdrew into himself and hid behind a negativistic attitude. When work assignments were given out, he refused to do them. When he was asked to do things, he replied with an insipid grin that he did not understand how to do them, or asked to be excused to see other staff members.

He is not liked by the other boys. He provokes them by calling them names, kicking them under the table, and so on. They have given him numerous nicknames, of which "The Sneak" and "The Snitch" are the most complimentary.

He has shown some academic progress, especially in arithmetic. However, he still functions below his age and grade level.

Final report. Isaac has improved considerably during the past two months. He has adjusted to the classroom structure, participated willingly in group functions, and completed his work assignments without pressure from me. Apparently his relationships with the other boys have improved because he is less provocative. However, the other boys still dislike him and poke fun at him. His academic functioning is still more than a year below his grade level.

Psychotherapist's Report (New Therapist)

Isaac tended to be relatively quiet during the interviews. When he did talk, he usually demanded something. He tried to use me in an attempt to avoid restrictions that the cottage parents had placed on him. He complained that they stole money from him and that he was sure they hated him, but he spoke of these things with lack of emotion.

He was moderately provocative with me, though not as much as the material in his record had indicated. He refused to leave the office at the end of interviews. In the beginning, I had to eject him forcibly. I was quite firm with him, and he became lesss provocative. There was a general apathy about this youngster which made him difficult to reach. At times while I was talking to him he wandered about the room, looked at the wall, and laughed to himself as though lost in a dream.

I discussed him with his cottage parents, who saw him as a provocative, manipulative, untrustworthy, and lazy youngster. He has successfully provoked them over a long period of time. As a result, they have developed a negative attitude toward him and have been firm to the point of being rigid and punitive with him. When his cottage parents tell him to do something, he just sits there, pretending he has not heard them. It is important that I clarify with Isaac his passive resistance and the hostility it involves. He often refuses to work when they tell him to. Then when they put pressure on him, he complains that they are treating him unfairly.

He recently asked me to change the time of our sessions because he wanted to avoid work assignments in the cottage. We talked at length about his relationship with his cottage parents. He said he hated them and often, under his breath, told them to drop dead. Then he asked me if I could fire them. I told him, "No." He said he did not mind working when it was his own idea, but that he resented having to work when others told him to. I asked him what his problem was with his cottage parents. He said that his cottage father was perfect and wanted him to be perfect, too. He stated that he was not going to be perfect. I then asked him about his good behavior in school. He replied, "Oh, that's different. I like school. That's why I behave."

At present he seems to be unable to express his hostility except in these indirect ways.

Report of the Leader of the Groupwork Program to Which He Had Been Assigned

Isaac seems to lack any real self-identity. Instead of acting on his own feelings, he mimics the characteristics of other people. In many ways his behavior has been an imitation of mine. For a while he kept group records as I did, reiterated my interpretations of the other boys' actions to them as if they were his own, and asked me for a list of the psychology books I read. He even succeeded in becoming the leader of the group, although he did not seem to derive much satisfaction from the role.

During the first few months of the program he was extremely "good." He spent much of his energy trying to anticipate what I might want him to do. During the last few weeks his behavior has become less artificial and he has been able to act out his "bad" feelings to some extent. However, he still cannot go too far in this respect because he is too frightened of exposing himself.

On several occasions, Isaac tried to instigate conflicts between me and other staff members, especially his teachers and his therapist. I told him that he was trying to use me to express his hostility for him. My conversations about this idea seemed to have had little effect on his behavior. Recently, I had to send him back to class when I found out that he had left class not to come to the group but to irritate his teacher.

III

HIGH SCHOOL PROGRAM: AGE 15

School Report: Social Studies and English Teacher (Male)

Initial report: November. Isaac's grades reflect the fact that he is probably the hardest worker in the class. However, he is in the process of solving some important problems:

1. When he first came into the class, he was very miserly. He hoarded pencils, paper, paper clips, and flaunted his sur-

pluses in front of the others when they were lacking in supplies. He has improved in this respect.

2. He demanded constant personal attention and called out answers before others had their chance. He has made considerable progress in this area as well.

3. He is constantly striving for an "A+." Marks are the most important thing to him, even more important than learning. He acts as if the reason for his being in the classroom is solely to earn a high grade rather than to learn interesting or useful information. When he does not earn 100, he is quite disappointed and wants to know the correct answer so that he can achieve 100 the next time.

4. He refuses to write anything but factual, descriptive compositions even when pressured. He evinces a complete lack of creative ability.

Although his reading difficulty does not seem to interfere with his studies, he should have remedial reading instruction.

Spring report. Isaac's attitude toward his peers has changed. He is not as miserly as he used to be and occasionally offers his supplies to students who need them. This partially helps to explain why his peers no longer tease him.

Isaac surprised me because I in no way anticipated that he would earn the highest grades in the class. However, despite his high grades, he is still anxious about his work and continually presses me for extra help and extra credit assignments.

Isaac is a very slow and careful worker. If rushed, his work deteriorates considerably. He reacts too strongly to competition because he wants to show the class that he knows all the right answers. He is justifiably proud of his academic achievements. Isaac seems to be ready to attend a regular school.

Final report. Isaac has completed the ninth grade in my class. His marks in social studies and English will be in the 90's. However, despite these high grades, there are still a number of unsolved problems facing him:

1. He is constantly striving for perfection, is dissatisfied with every mark under 100, and reacts initially to his errors as if they were mine.

2. He is so competitive in the classroom that the other students get angry. He especially likes to tell the students who have done poorly about how well he has done.

3. Either he enjoys provoking me, or he is extremely insensitive to my feelings. He is always demanding and insisting. He almost refuses to take "No" for an answer and believes that I am unfair if I do not yield to his demands.

4. He has very poor study habits. His notebook is a complete and utter hodgepodge. Everything is so disorganized, ripped, and out of place that I wonder how he can ever find anything at all.

5. He still gives the appearance of being much more interested in grades than in acquiring knowledge.

6. He still works very slowly and methodically, and is always behind the rest of the class when we work together as a group.

7. He sets his standards by what the teacher expects of him rather than by what he might expect from himself. His usual approach to goal setting is to find out what I consider to be the best, and then to strive to reach that level.

8. Isaac has improved somewhat in his ability to choose between alternatives, but indecision is still one of his major problems.

9. His ability to do creative writing has been tapped recently by his writing a poem and a few short stories. However, he still exhibits a lack of imagination and an unwillingness to express himself. Most of his compositions are very factual and unimaginative.

10. He relies excessively on rote memory.

Isaac claims that he has no outside interests and his actions in class reflect his belief that his only interest in life is to earn high grades. He would do much better in the class if he could find another source of satisfaction.

Science and Math Teacher (Male)

Initial report. Isaac is showing a fantastic amount of interest in his schoolwork. However, he still has one major difficulty: he cannot sit still and constantly comes up to me for help, when with a little thought, he could figure out the problem for himself. He attempts to monopolize my time in this way.

He gets along with the other students, but is quick to report their transgressions to me.

Mid-year report. Isaac is a conscientious and hard worker who is extremely methodical in everything he does. He works very slowly and is often behind the rest of the class. He cannot think about obvious problems and wants every point and detail personally explained to him. On many occasions I have refused to do this. Even if a problem is worked out and carefully explained in the book, he comes up and asks for help without studying the example. He also has a terrible habit of leaning on me whenever I explain something to him. He asks questions during a lecture period that have already been answered. His work is excellent, but much too compulsive. He needs constant encouragement. He often provokes his peers.

Final report. Isaac is not very well liked by the other members of the class. As a matter of fact, I myself cannot stand him. He has a mannerism about him that invites criticism from others. He has a tendency to antagonize me by the things that he says, and in the way he behaves. He tends to look down on others, questioning them in the minutest detail. He makes quite a pest of himself in this way. I am not complaining about his intellectual curiosity, but I am questioning the method by which he seeks to satisfy it. He refuses to take "No" for an answer, and he continually irritates and pesters me by asking me the same question until I am almost at my wits' end!

Isaac has a highly competitive attitude toward his schoolwork, and studies much more than anyone else. He probably memorizes his assignments in his science textbook, for he seems to have committed even the most minute items to memory.

It is difficult for Isaac to learn. It is with a sheer compulsive perseverance that he is able to succeed in his academic work. His average mark on the past five science tests is 95. As I have already said, he puts most of his emphasis on memory and persistent, constant study in the cottage.

Although he is an exceptionally hard worker in math, Isaac finds it rather difficult to understand mathematical processes. He often comes to me for help before he has read the instructions in his workbook. Even after I have explained the process to him, he may return to his seat only to appear at my desk once more with the same question. He may return five or six times with the same question before he finally understands the process. On several occasions I have refused to help him when I sensed that he had not read the instructions carefully and had not attempted to think the problem out for himself. I recall one particular incident which occurred several weeks ago when Isaac was studying areas of geometric figures. I had explained to him at least half a dozen times that square means multiply the number by itself, and pointed out the formula in his book. However, he kept multiplying each item by two because he would not take the time to look up the formula, which was plainly printed on the page. Later, we turned to the exercises about finding the area of a circle. Again he kept asking me how to find the area. Even after I had circled the formula for him in the book, he still had difficulty in grasping the method.

Although I have been rather sharp and pointed in my criticism of Isaac in front of the class, he still reacts in a rather positive way toward me. It has been only recently that he has become aware of my exasperation with him. Now, when he comes to my desk with a question, he says, "Don't get mad now, John, don't think that this is a silly question, but . . . ." Isaac is becoming more aware of the fact that I am trying to make him stand on his own two feet and he has been showing some improvement recently.

There is no doubt in my mind that Isaac could complete high school, and probably college, if he were to develop his potential.

Psychotherapist's Final Summary

In the early fall, Isaac was hostile and uncooperative in the cottage. He used passive resistance with his cottage parents. He worked slowly, acted defiantly, refused to cooperate, and attempted to use his religion to avoid work. Because he was not required to do the housework chores on the Sabbath, he was asked to do them on an alternate day. He initially resented this alternate-day work, felt he should not do it, and was generally hostile and resistant to any attempts by his cottage parents to have him do it.

In the cottage, Isaac was a lone wolf who had no close relationship with any of the other boys. However, he slowly began to develop positive feelings toward his cottage parents. He began working better and more cooperatively, and made less effort to use his religion to avoid work. Before his discharge, he began to volunteer to work on another day in order to make up for the work he had missed on the Sabbath. At these times he often did more than the other boys had done. Although he was never able to develop close relationships with his peers in the cottage, he became less aggressive and thus, less troublesome to them.

At the beginning of the school year, he behaved in a hostile, smart-aleck way, talked back to the teacher, and often disrupted the class. After a while he began to take his studies more seriously. He spent long hours in the cottage in methodical study. This helped him to earn high grades, but it also isolated him from the other boys in the cottage. His improved academic functioning was accompanied by a decrease in his hyperactivity, an improvement in his relationships with the other students in the class, and a lessening of his suspicions about his teachers. At present, he would like to finish high school, complete college, and teach vocational arts.

Toward the end of his stay at the institution, he was permitted to visit his home more frequently in order to plan for his return to the community. He appears to follow his mother's wishes completely without thinking for himself. She swore him to secrecy and he refused to discuss his plans for the future with anyone at the institution. It was not until we received a letter of inquiry from a school he was planning to attend did we learn what he had decided to do.

Isaac is still a seriously disturbed boy. He is suspicious, guarded, especially afraid of close contacts with adults. He is a very demanding youngster whose hostile impulses lie just below the surface. He has found a few areas of satisfaction, especially achievement in school. He has learned to control some of his inner turmoil through a rather compulsive, methodical approach toward the world. This has been an important factor in his school achievement.

QUESTIONS ABOUT THE CASE STUDY

1. In which dimensions of personality did Isaac have major problems?
2. What educational difficulties did these problems create?
3. How might an educator deal with them?
4. In which category of emotional disturbance does Isaac belong?
5. What modifications would Isaac have required in terms of appropriate teacher-pupil relationship, course content and method of presentation, class size, and grouping during his final year at the institution?
6. In what ways did Isaac's teachers' own problems interfere with their handling of his difficulties?

QUESTIONS FOR FURTHER THOUGHT
AND DISCUSSION

The Students

The situations included in this section are offered as an exercise in understanding a student's educational difficulties in terms of his underlying problems. The situations were chosen because they represent difficulties often encountered by educators of emotionally disturbed students and because each of them can result from a number of different underlying problems.

In each situation, form a hypothesis about the motivations and dynamics which might have led each of the students cited to behave as described; think of the personality characteristics of each student which might influence your decision on how to handle the difficulty with him; and decide on an approach to follow with each student. Discuss each situation as if you were one of the students' teachers during their stay at the institution.

1. At the outset of the class you notice that one of the students has taken a seat in the back row instead of his regular one and seems to be involved in his own thoughts. (Joan and Ralph)

2. After half of the class period has passed, a student states that he will be unable to complete the examination during the class time. (Deborah and Isaac)

3. A student refuses to complete an assignment in a social studies unit about tariffs which involves mathematical concepts. He says that he does not care to learn about it because it will never be useful to him. (Deborah and Ralph)

4. A student refuses to begin work on an examination which you have just handed out. He claims that the questions are unfair because they do not cover the aspects which were important in the work he studied. Then he asks to be given another day to prepare himself. (Deborah, Joan, and Ralph)

5. During the second term a student asks you to give him an extra credit assignment. (Deborah, Ralph, and Isaac)

6. During a discussion in the biology class about diseases which result from vitamin deficiencies, a student begins to ask questions which are only tangential to the topic at hand. (Deborah, Joan, and Ralph)

7. Almost immediately after you have handed out some new material for the students to read in class, one of them informs you that he wants to be excused from class because he cannot understand the materials. (Joan and Ralph)

The Educator

1. Which, if any, of the problems of the teachers in the case studies remind you of some of your own classroom difficulties?

2. How would your own problems have interfered in your relationships with each of the students?

References

BERKOWITZ, P. H., and ESTHER ROTHMAN. *The disturbed child*. New York: New York University Press, 1960.

BETTELHEIM, B. *Love is not enough*. New York: The Free Press of Glencoe, 1949.

BRENNER, C. *An elementary textbook of psychoanalysis*. New York: International Universities Press, 1955.

COHEN, A. *Delinquent boys*. New York: The Free Press of Glencoe, 1955.

CRUICKSHANK, W. M., FRANCES A. BENTZEN, MARION T. TANNHAUSER, and F. H. RATZEBURG. *A teaching method for brain injured and hyperactive children*. Syracuse, N. Y.: Syracuse University Press, 1961.

CUTTS, NORMA E., and N. MOSELEY. *Teaching the disorderly pupil in elementary and secondary school*. New York: David McKay Company, Inc., 1957.

DEVEREUX, G. *Therapeutic education*. New York: Harper & Row, 1956.

177

DOLLARD, J., and N. E. MILLER. *Personality and psychotherapy.* New York: McGraw-Hill Book Company, Inc., 1950.

DOSTOEVSKY, F. "The gambler." In *The short novels of Dostoevsky.* New York: Dial Press, 1945.

DOSTOEVSKY, F. "Notes from the underground." In *The short novels of Dostoevsky.* New York: Dial Press, 1945.

FENICHEL, C. "An elementary school for seriously disturbed children," in *New steps to mental health.* New York: Bulletin of Brooklyn Council for Social Planning, 1953, pp. 25–27.

FREUD, ANNA. *The ego and the mechanisms of defense.* London: Hogarth Press, Ltd., 1937.

FREUD, S. *The psychopathology of everyday life.* New York: The Macmillan Company, 1914.

FREUD, S. *The problem of anxiety.* New York: W. W. Norton & Company, Inc., 1936.

FREUD, S. *An outline of psychoanalysis.* New York: W. W. Norton & Company, Inc., 1949.

FROMM, E. The art of loving. New York: Harper & Row, 1956.

GOLDFARB, W. *Childhood schizophrenia.* Cambridge, Mass.: Harvard University Press, 1961.

GOLDSMITH, J. M., H. KROHN, RUTH OCHROCH, and N. KAGAN. "Changing the delinquent's concept of school." *Amer. J. Orthopsychiat.,* 1959, *29,* 249–265.

GOLDSMITH, J. M., RENA SCHULMAN, and H. GROSSBARD. "Integrating clinical processes with planned living experiences," in G. L. Gorlow and W. Katkovsky (Eds.), *Readings in the psychology of adjustment.* New York: McGraw-Hill Book Company, Inc., 1959.

GOLDSTEIN, K. and M. SCHEERER. "Abstract and concrete behavior: An experimental study with special tests." *Psychol. Monogr.,* 1941, *53,* No. 239.

HARING, N. G., and E. L. PHILLIPS. *Educating emotionally disturbed children.* New York: McGraw-Hill Book Company, Inc., 1962.

HIRSCHBERG, J. C. "The role of education in the treatment of emotionally disturbed children through planned ego development." *Amer. J. Orthopsychiat.*, 1953, *23*, 684–690.

JACOBSON, S., and C. FALGRE. "Neutralization: A tool for the teacher of disturbed children." *Except. Child.*, 1959, *25*, 243–246.

JERSILD, A. T. *Child psychology.* Englewood Cliffs, N. J.: Prentice-Hall, Inc., 1960.

MAY, R. *The meaning of anxiety.* New York: The Ronald Press Company, 1950.

MENNINGER, K. *Theory of psychoanalytic technique.* New York: Science Editions, 1961.

MUNROE, RUTH L. *Schools of psychoanalytic thought.* New York: Holt, Rinehart and Winston, Inc., 1955.

NEILL, A. S. *Summerhill: A radical approach to child rearing.* New York: Hart Publishing Company, 1960.

NEWMAN, RUTH G. "The acting out boy." *Except. Child.*, 1956, *22*, 186–190, 204–216.

PEARSON, G. H. J. *Emotional disorders of children.* New York: W. W. Norton & Company, Inc., 1949.

PEARSON, G. H. J. *Psychoanalysis and the education of the child.* New York: W. W. Norton & Company, Inc., 1954.

PIAGET, J. *The origins of intelligence in children.* New York: International Universities Press, 1952.

POLSKY, H. W. *Cottage six.* New York: Russell Sage Foundation, 1962.

RABINOW, B. "The role of the school in residental treatment." *Amer. J. Orthopsychiat.*, 1955, *25*, 685–691.

RAPAPORT, D. (Ed.) *Organization and pathology of thought.* New York: Columbia University Press, 1951.

REDL, F., and D. WINEMAN. *The aggressive child.* New York: The Free Press of Glencoe, 1957.

REICH, W. *Character analysis.* Rangeley, Me.: Orgone Institute Press, 1949.

ROGERS, C. R. *Client-centered therapy.* Boston: Houghton Mifflin Company, 1951.

SHAFFER, L. F., and E. J. SHOBEN, JR. *The psychology of adjustment.* Boston: Houghton Mifflin Company, 1956.

SULLIVAN, H. S. *The interpersonal theory of psychiatry.* New York: W. W. Norton & Company, Inc., 1953.

SYKES, G. M., and D. MATZA. "Techniques of neutralization: A theory of delinquency." *Amer. Sociol. Rev.,* 1957, *22,* 664–670.

WHITE, R. W. *The abnormal personality.* New York: The Ronald Press Company, 1964.

index